The defence of a position selected as a field of battle

Thomas Fraser, Royal Engineer Prize Essay. 1875

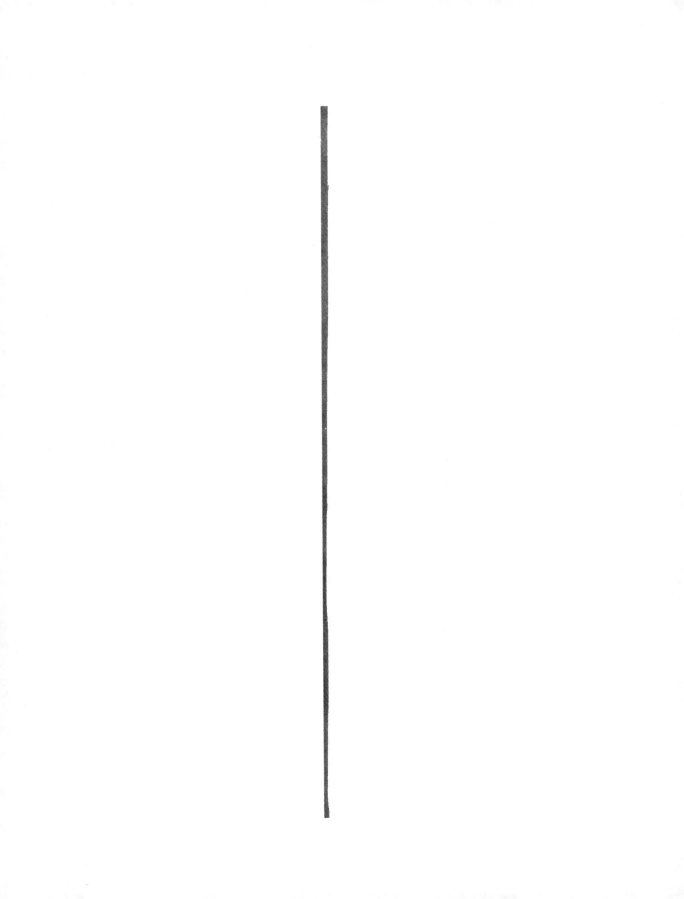

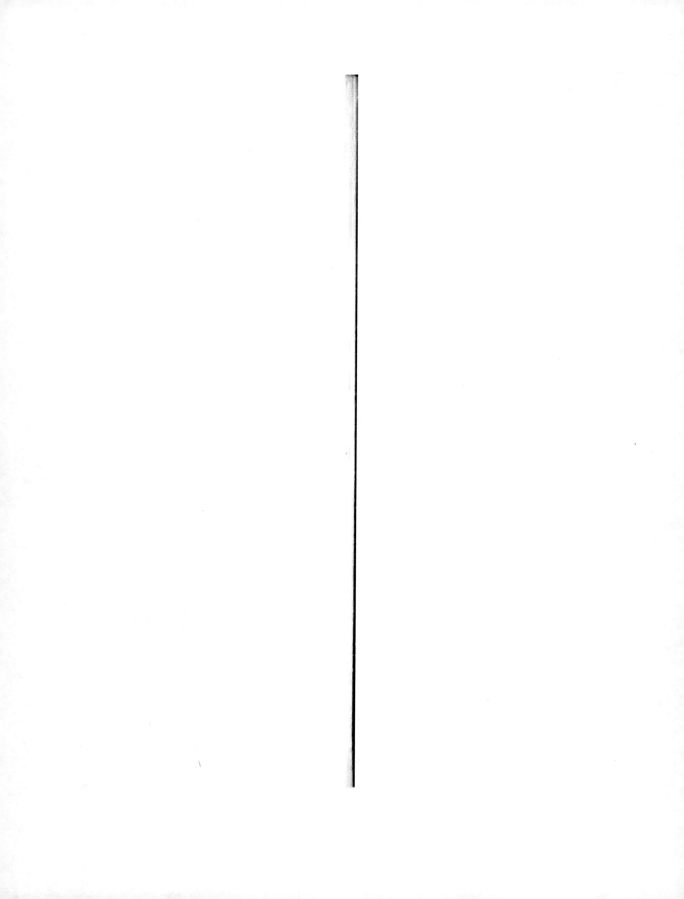

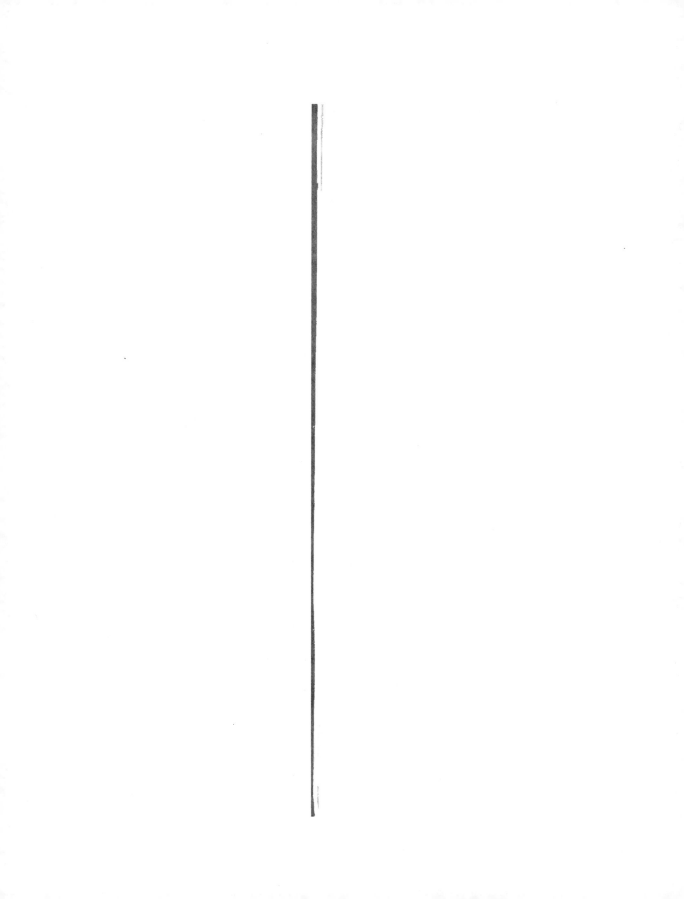

ROYAL ENGINEER PRIZE ESSAY

FOR 1875.

THE DEFENCE OF A POSITION

SELECTED AS

A FIELD OF BATTLE.

BY

CAPTAIN T. FRASER, R.E.

CONDITIONS OF ESSAY FOR 1875.

The occupation of a position selected as a field of battle, and the means to be taken to strengthen and prepare it under various conditions of occupation, such as more or less time for the construction of works, and greater or less proximity to the enemy, including the possibility of immediate attack, the ground being taken up in his presence.

The conditions should be stated which determine the position for the Artillery, also the occupation of adjacent villages, farms, enclosures, woods, &c, the readiest means of turning these and such other natural or artificial objects, as woods, railways, rivers, &c., as are ordinarily met with, to the best account, should also be stated.

The Essay should contain a discussion as to the least number of troops of the various arms requisite for the defence of a given position.

All general principles should be illustrated, when possible, by reference to examples from actual warfare.

The nature of works should be described, and, when necessary, explained by sketches with figured dimensions

The usual appliances which accompany a well equipped modern army in the field, are to be considered available for the purpose of the Essay.

The length of the Essay should not exceed 24 pages of the Professional Papers of the Corps of Royal Engineers.

Essays to be sent in by the 31st of March, 1875.

ERRATA.

Page 11, line 35, for " manœuvring" read " manœuvering."

Page 12, line 21, for " Carrière" read " Carrières."

Page 12, line 35, for " manœuvring" read " manœuvering."

Page 12, Foot Note ‡ for " Crossay" read " Croissy."

Page 13, line 28, for " lie" read " lay."

Page 15, Foot Note ‡ for " Lœlein" read " Löhlein."

Page 16, Foot Note * after " légion " read " du Rhône " and
         général Cremer."

Page 16, Foot Note ‖ for " face" read " pace."

Page 20, Foot Note ‡ for " Henri" read " Henry."

Page 22, line 21, for " Vaudois" read " Vaudois."

Page 22, Foot Note § for " Lœlein" read " Löhlein."

Page 23, Foot Note † for " Henri" read " Henry."

Page 23, Foot Note ‡ for " Lœlein" read " Löhlein."

Page 23, Foot Note † for " Lœlein" read " Löhlein."

Page 27, Foot Note * for " Wissemberg" read " Weissemberg."

Pl. vii. Note to Fig. 47, for " (Ai to B)" read " (Ai to A.)"

159.

[Tout jours prest.]

THE DEFENCE OF A POSITION, SELECTED AS A FIELD OF BATTLE.

"Du gehst nicht weg, dann geht der feind weg."—*Boguslawski.*

The question of the defence of positions is a constantly recurring one in the history of war, because, of two forces in the field, it generally happens that one is driven or led to act on the defensive, either from inferiority of any kind alone, or with a view to gain or maintain some strategetical or other advantage. In saying this, we admit, in general, that the force capable of taking the offensive is the one more likely to succeed in obtaining decisive results · what we are concerned with, is rather to consider when the defensive is desirable or unavoidable, and how, under these circumstances, it can be used most successfully.

OBJECTS OF THE DEFENSIVE

In speaking of cases in which the defender aims at a decisive result, that is, at crushing the attack on the battlefield, we shall refer to his tactics as "*Offensive-defensive*" while, if his main object be attained by simply holding his position, the action is called a *covering action* Even in this case, however, a purely passive defence is rarely advisable, though the extent to which offensive returns can be carried out, is usually limited by want of numbers.

OFFENSIVE-DEFENSIVE ACTIONS.

A commander most often decides on offensive-defensive action when, with a force about equal or not much inferior to his opponent, he can find an offensive position which either bars or threatens the hostile advance, and at the same time so favourable for defence, that the lesser part of his forces can be trusted to shatter the assailant, while it lets him strike in force at the moment of reaction, and push his success.

Such were some of our battles in Spain, where, under a chief, whose knowledge of fire tactics was far in advance of that of his contemporaries, the assailant's shock was stopped by fire and repulsed by a counter stroke. In the Peninsula, however, the fire contest was most often shortlived, and the infantry line, after a few rounds, frequently took the offensive, while with the new arms, the forward advance of the *shooting line* has become both difficult and questionable, and the counter attack is more often made by reserves held in hand for the purpose.

COVERING ACTIONS.

The following appear to be the circumstances which most often lead to covering actions in a defended position, namely :—

(1) When the position is meant to cover important points on lines of communication.

(2). When it covers the capital or some important town, magazine, or arsenal.

(3). When a circle of investment is prepared defensively.

(4). When a force is called upon to cover the operations of a siege which the enemy threatens to interrupt or raise.

(5).   When the position covers part of the front of an army acting offensively.

(6).   When a garrison is enabled, by occupying advanced defensive positions, to hold the enemy at a greater distance from the fortress.

(7).   When a rear guard holds a position to cover a retreat.

Defence of Communications.

Under the first head, cases will occur, as for instance at important passages of rivers, or in the defence of defiles where the enemy's aim, and, consequently, the line of his advance, is defined within small limits ; and where also the defender may have the great advantage of placing both flanks in security from turning movements : this relieves him from the necessity of extreme extension, and short lines, strongly fortified, seem suitable, provided that their situation be such as to prevent the hostile artillery from occupying positions whence its fire could reach the communications.

Defence of Strategic Points.

In the second case, the force covering a town or arsenal must hold a position sufficiently advanced, and, therefore, extended, to prevent an assailant from in-flicting serious injury by means of his distant artillery fire, without being driven to risk an assault.   The position prepared and taken up by the French army of the Loire (war of 1870-71) to cover the arsenal of Bourges, to a certain extent, fulfilled these conditions, and alone, according to Gœtze, prevented its capture by the Germans.

These two first cases of covering actions often take place in positions prepared beforehand, with a view to possible retreat, which frequently take the form of *intrenched camps* on sites of strategical importance, at which reserves and ma-terials may be collected, and under cover of which, troops, which have been worsted, may re-organise and recruit.   The camp at Chalons was intended to be, and was not, so used in the war of 1870-71.   In the case of an invasion, such positions, even if they do not compel attack, at least narrow the lines of the in-vader's advance, and cause him to lose time or incur risk in passing them.   In the latter case both intrenched camps and *manœuvring bridge-heads* are used as strategical pivots for the field army, and should be prepared offensively.   On the other hand, an invader may prepare similar positions to secure his line of opera-tions and prevent disaster.*

The Defence of Lines of Investment.

Of all classes of defensive actions, none seem to have received so extraordinary a development in the war of 1870-71 as those in which, not only garrisons, but great field armies, have been shut within their fortresses, and there held till the excess of their own numbers compelled them to surrender.   History records no events of the kind which even approach those of the surrender of Metz and Paris since the days that Cæsar in the same country, and with a force only 70,000 strong, enclosed Vercinjetorix in Alesia, and in 70 days compelled his surrender with 80,000 men.

The peculiarities of these investing operations are, that the investing force must, at the commencement, act energetically on the offensive, so as to secure a circle of defensive positions on as short a circumference as possible, and to gain time for preparation ; after which the force so shut in can only act by taking the offensive, and that too *without* the power of making flank attacks.

The defensive preparations for investment are often made more easy by the railways which converge on the town, and by the number and excellence of the roads in the neighbourhood.   To these advantages may be added the small sub-divisions of land and the number of houses, enclosures, villages, parks, &c., which are commonly found about great cities.

* In the campaign of 1813, Napoleon fortified Dresden as an intrenched camp, and Pirna as a bridge head : the works round Kars in 1854 also formed an intrenched camp.

The Covering of a Siege.

In actions fought to cover a siege or investment, the covering troops look to those of the investing force to retain the garrison. The most favourable covering position may often be at a considerable distance from the place, but, in any case, entirely out of the reach of its guns, and so far from the investing line, that the latter may be in no way affected by the artillery fire of the attack. †

Offensive use of Defences.

In recent wars, while the defender has had, more than ever, to use the offensive to secure success, the assailant has constantly had to keep the defensive in view : thus the great importance of flank attacks has led occasionally to the fortifying of part of the front of an army on the offensive, preparatory to an attack made from a flank. ‡ This was particularly the case in the late American war, towards the close of which the combatants had acquired considerable skill both in manœuvring and in using intrenchments.

Field Defence by the Besieged.

At the beginning of a siege, the besieger is forced to draw the line of investment at a considerable distance from the fortress ; and if, in addition, an active defender holds a prepared position within the range of the place, the investing line is still further thrust out along its front, and the difficulties and delays that occur are much increased. In this case the fortress affords to the defender a secure base, while its guns support his position and render it extremely difficult for the attack to press home an assault on it. Thus the protracted defence of Belfort (1870-71) was due, in a great measure, to the line of defended villages (Danjoutin, Pérouse, &c.) occupied for some time by the French, for the capture of which night attacks had to be resorted to.

Action of a Rear-Guard.

The great increase in retaining power afforded by the breech-loader has directly increased the efficiency of a rear-guard. Rear-guard actions have this peculiarity, that they are often, though not always, fought with the object of holding the position for a short time only, in which case special thought must be given to the lines of retreat and to the means of covering them.

MODERN DEFENSIVE TACTICS.

The above considerations (chiefly strategical) are generally as applicable to former wars as to those of the immediate future. They have been entered into to show the extent of defensive action and the modifications that are caused by circumstances. When, however, we come to the tactical management of the defence, we find that a change in the method of fighting has, as usual, followed the changes in arms. The effect of rifled field guns began to be felt in 1859, while in 1866 the power of the breech-loader was established beyond all doubt ; but, in the latter case particularly, the German superiority in all points, except perhaps in artillery tactics, was so marked, that success was not entirely due to the arm. In the campaign of 1870-71, however, the opposing forces were for the first time armed with the new weapon. Hence this campaign alone can be considered as a true index of what we have now to expect, and no excuse is wanted for drawing mainly upon it, and upon the conclusions come to by the actors in it, for the consideration of our subject.

† In the war of 1870-71 the battles at Bapaume and on the Lisaine were fought to cover the sieges of Peronne and Belfort.

‡ This use of defences differs from the offensive-defensive, for in the latter the offensive generally follows, while in the former it may precede defensive action.

Causes qualifying the conclusions from the War of 1870-71.

There are, however, a few reservations to be made in accepting these conclusions. In the first place, national vanity generally* leads each country to believe that the more brilliant rôle of the attack is best fitted for the genius of its soldiers. For this cause, prejudice is apt to incline the balance of opinion in favour of the attack, while success on the offensive is more often set down to individual superiority than to that of numbers and organization, which in 1870 were really among the main causes. Again, in this campaign the infantry arm of the Germans was much inferior in shooting power to that of the French, and to those now in use in the armies of Europe, and this has, perhaps, led them rather to under-rate the distance of the most effective infantry fire, a distance which, though limited by the range of distinct vision, we may expect to see somewhat increased when the newest armaments come into action.†

With these reservations, however, we are bound to accept the teachings of experience; and though in our campaigns against inferior races, where daring is perhaps the chief element of success, we need not always be bound to the latest European tactics, still, the tactics which are found to be the best under the most trying conditions, cannot fail, if wisely modified, to be the same under those of less difficulty.

Captain May's criticisms in the "Tactical retrospect" on the action of the artillery and engineer services in 1866 (for which they should be ever grateful), were shewn, in 1870, to have borne fruit in bringing them both to the front.

Again, with reference to the investing works round Paris in 1870-71, we find another infantry officer remark, "The works directed by engineer officers, however excellent they may have been with regard to their technical execution, did not always show that these officers had, so to say, understood how to reduce to practice the tactical ideas of the present time."‡ Such an opinion justifies us in giving great prominence to the tactical considerations that bear on the subject, and we cannot do better than commence by examining the mechanism of the attack for which the defence has to prepare.

Formations for Attack.

Although our field exercises do not define very exactly what our formations for attack should be,§ what concerns us more in this case is, that in the great continental armies, a certain uniformity of opinion seems to have been arrived at as the result of recent experience.

Owing to the great difficulty of a direct advance against the breech-loader, the attacking force will now most often endeavour to use its superiority by trying to turn one or both flanks of the position, || while holding the front, by an attack which should keep the defender's troops opposed to it, from extending to, or reinforcing the flanks. This attack may not be pushed home till that on the flank or flanks has struck. The assailant plainly puts his strength to the best use when he so times his attack that he engages the whole of the defender's line at once. With increased extension, however, this is now less easy, and in the war

---

* Our Peninsular experience has rather inclined us to the defensive in European wars.

† We must remember, too, that the Germans only used common shell with percussion fuzes, while the French time fuzes both for common and shrapnel were meant only for two ranges.

‡ Boguslawski, "Taktische Folgerungen aus dem Feldzuge 1870-71;" translated by Graham.

§ Since writing the above, very clear and concise regulations for the attack have been issued for use in the Manœuvres of 1875.

|| The way in which the assailant's masses are now often made to converge on to the battle field makes this more easy. Thus at Königgratz, Le Mans, &c.

of 1870-71, it was often the case that the advanced guard of a brigade or division was seriously engaged before the general attack began.* In all cases the actual advance will be more or less *frontal* even when directed on a flank, and the main ideas of such an attack seem to be. †

1st. Preparation for the infantry advance by a powerful concentric artillery fire in order to shake and paralyze the defender, and to destroy material obstacles.

2nd. Preparation for the assault, by infantry in *individual order*, which attempts, by its fire, at effective musketry range, to overcome the defender's power of resistance.

3rd. The advance to the assault of the same infantry, backed up by its reserves.

This use of the individual order gives the attack the greatest mobility and security from fire while developing its own fire to the utmost. After the fight has been opened by the reconnaissances which the assailant must make to get information and to gain time for consideration, for the giving of orders and the preparation for turning movements (all of which must be arranged at this stage and not later), the advancing columns deploy as they approach the zone of the defender's artillery fire, which, under conditions favourable to its use, may extend as far as 3,000 yards from the position, though the ground, fog, mist, &c., may often lessen this distance. ‡

The assailant's artillery comes into action at about this range, and will probably have to make one or two advances during the fight. In doing so it strives to place itself so that it may continue its support to the attacking infantry up to the moment of the assault; § while at each stage of the attack it aims at diverting the defender's fire as much as possible from the infantry to itself, using at the same time every accident of ground, &c., which can give it cover. ||

The attacking line of infantry is divided into:—

(1) Shooting line; (2) Supports; (3) Main body.

The supports may sometimes be as strong as the shooting line, but rarely less than half the latter, and the two together are from one-fourth to one-half of the whole force. In order to get the maximum effective fire, the men in the shooting line are as close together as they can be, so as to move and shoot; namely, each occupying about $1\frac{1}{2}$ paces.

Thus a battalion of 1,000 men, with two or three companies in the shooting

---

* At Spicheren, for example. At the battle of Belfort, too, one cause of failure was that the attacks along the line were so isolated and ill-timed, that the defender was allowed to shift his reserves from place to place, as each was threatened in succession.

† The analogy between the attack of a position and of a fortress is well pointed out in Gen. Ducrot's late pamphlet, "Instruction des Tirailleurs." He says, "We think the general's art has much analgoy with that of the engineer." The difference between the art of the engineer and that of the general being, that the one is opposed to the work of years; the other to that of hours.

‡ Thus the French, in attacking Hericourt (battle of Belfort, 1871), on the 16th of January, were enabled, under cover of a dense fog, to get close up to the town. On the other hand, the late trials at Dartmoor (1875), point to the probability of even longer effective ranges. Thus the 16-pounder water and Shrapnel shells made an average of 14 hits each, on targets representing a column of squadrons, at 4,000 yards (known) range, with percussion fuzes only; the 9 seconds T fuze being only good for about 3,000 yards; at the latter range, Shrapnel with T fuze averaged four to six hits per shell on a half battalion column target.

§ At the attack of the village of Chénebier (battle of Belfort, 1871), it is mentioned in "Le General Crémer" that the French artillery ceased fire when their infantry got up to within 1,200 metres of the Germans; and the French lost 1,100 men in driving two battalions out of the village. At St. Privat, on the contrary, the German guns fired on the village *after* their infantry got in.

|| At the same battle the French, during the attack, intrenched a number of field guns by the Mont Chevis Farm, whence their fire silenced some German field guns in the open.—Von der Wengen (Die Kampfe vor Belfort).

line, would give a front of about 350 to 550 paces, according to the cover available.

Nature of Fire bearing on the Attack

In advancing from deployment, the infantry first enters the zone of the defender's unaimed musketry fire at from 1,000 to 1,200 yards from the position. In crossing this zone to that of his aimed fire (500 to 700 yards from the position), speed alone saves loss * and the nature of formation does not much affect it, except when aimed fire is kept up, as it often will be, at very long ranges ; when, of course, large compact bodies suffer most. in any case the defender's artillery fire will prevent the use of large bodies, if exposed.

In crossing the zone of aimed fire, the advance of the main body is only possible owing to the fact that though the defender would gain most by firing on the main body and supports, he is sure to be tempted into firing mostly on the shooting line, while his guns may be drawn to fire on those of the attack.

Advance of the Shooting Line.

The shooting line moves through the zone of unaimed fire, firing, if at all, by word of command. On reaching the zone of aimed fire, they advance by alternate fractions in rushes of 50 to 60 paces, the fraction not in motion keeping up fire to cover the rush When the line gets up to the most effective range,† it commences rapid independent firing Formerly the decision of a fight was said to rest on the fact that two hostile bodies could not at the same time occupy the same space. Now-a-days it appears that they cannot both *hold on* under fire for many minutes, even when some hundred yards apart ‡ hence the crisis of the fire contest ends quickly, either by the repulse of the shooting line, now augmented by the supports, or by its rapid advance, supported by its main body, to the point of assault.

Advance of the Supports.

Up to the zone of aimed musketry fire, the supports follow the shooting line at say 300 paces distance. This distance seems most suitable, for while all musketry fire ranges considerably, it has been observed § that artillery fire is more accurate, and is more often low than high, so that when directed on one object, its effects do not extend much over 300 paces beyond ‖ As the supports feel the effects of the aimed fire, they form line, and then open line (files covering as they do not fire), spreading out and closing in as they best can. The supports feed the shooting line on which they close, as it gets to the position for rapid firing, and by the time the main body approaches, they will all have joined it.

Advance of the Main Body

Up to the unaimed fire zone, the main body advances in small shallow columns of from half to a quarter of a battalion. From this on, the defensive artillery fire makes it best to sub-divide further into bodies with a front of 30 to 40 paces, and

* Colonel Gawler, " The British line in the attack " von Scherff, " The new tactics of infantry ," translated by Graham

† Boguslawski puts this at from 500 to 150 paces , Von Scherff at from 400 to 200 paces from the defender's line.

‡ " Assuming, from the lessons of the late war, that a rapid independent fire from both sides, such as above supposed, cannot well last above five minutes, without bringing things to a crisis."—Scherff.

§ Scherff.

‖ Thus at 2,000 yards (known) with targets representing 100 men one pace apart, with 100 in support at 250 paces, and 200 as main body 600 paces in rear of them (the two latter in line two deep), 288 shells fired at the shooting line made 358 hits on it, and only 10 or 12 on the supports, and two or three on the main body.—Dartmoor, 1875

50 to 80 paces apart. Some of these, if much exposed, form open line, but get together again where cover permits. In order to be up in time for the assault, the main body will, at first, keep about 500 yards behind the skirmishers, so that when the latter commence the rapid firing, the main body will be within 250 to 350 yards of them. When the main body gets within about 50 yards of the skirmishers, the moment of the assault arrives, and the whole move forward, the main body aiming at the point of entry. Once in, they will endeavour to gain the further border of the defences, but will leave the conduct of a further advance to fresh troops.

Advance of the Artillery.

The divisional artillery will, in the meantime, have advanced with, or before, the main body to their final positions, at a distance of 1,000 to 1,500 yards from the defenders.[*]

Supporting Lines.

The attacking line, even when the front is short, will have troops in support. When the front is extensive, a small intermediate body, or *second* line, will follow 200 or 300 yards behind the main body, to fill up gaps that may occur, while a reserve, or *third* line ($\frac{1}{4}$th or $\frac{1}{3}$rd of the whole) follows at 400 to 500 yards in rear of the second line. Both these bodies help to protect the attacking line from counterstrokes, and, after the assault, the second clears the defender out of the captured works, while the third pushes further forward if need be.

ADVANTAGES OF THE OFFENSIVE.

The advantages claimed for the offensive are—

1st. That of the initiative, wherein its strength has always lain, which enables it to decide *when*, *where*, and *how* to strike. This is, however, to some extent limited by the judgment of the defender in choosing the position.[†]

2nd. That the attack has, with the new arms, an increased power of bringing a converging and cross fire on the defender's line, and particularly on the points of assault. In attacks on posts [‡] or small positions, the converging nature of its fire gives great power to the attack. When, however, the position is extensive, it only gets this advantage in so far as it can overlap the defender's flanks.

Much stress is laid on the effect of the preliminary artillery fire, and its moral effect on exposed troops is, no doubt, great. We must, however, remember that even in ordinary fights, the losses due to this fire are set down at only 1-12th or 1-13th of the whole;[§] so that against troops under cover the loss cannot be very great.

In the artillery engagement at long ranges there is, however, one point in favour of the attack when firing against intrenchments, namely, that at those ranges the angle of descent is considerable. Thus the drop of a 16-pdr. M.L.R. shell at 4,000 yards is roughly 15° or 1 in 4; at 3,000 yards it is almost 10° or 1 in 5·7; at 2,000 yards it is about $5\frac{2}{3}$° or 1 in 10; and at 1,000 yards about $2\frac{1}{4}$° or 1 in 28; while with the 9-pdr. M.R.L. the drop at 3,000 yards is over 1 in 5: hence the attack gains in searching power, and the defence loses in grazing power with direct fire at long ranges. In both cases, however, when it

[*] Capt. Hime, R.A. (R.A. prize essay), puts the limit of musketry fire against guns at 900 yards.

[†] "The defender possessed and still possesses a certain general initiative by means of which (if only his position be strategically good) he can, from the nature of the position taken up, attract his opponent and force him to advance in one or more directions determined by and known to him beforehand."—Von Scherff.

[‡] That on Le Bourget, for instance.—Paris, 1870—71.

[§] Home, "Précis of Modern Tactics."

is too far for the gunners to see * the effects, they are comparatively † slight. At the same time the successful use of curved fire in recent sieges, where the ranges were known, may lead to its use by the defence for searching out open spaces concealed by ground or woods, where the attacking troops may mass provided that the positions and ranges have been learned beforehand. The addition of the 64-pr. M.L. howitzer of 18 cwt, now under trial, as a gun of position, would make this the more easy (Fig. 29, Pl. VI.)

3rd. That infantry can now load and fire in any position (a gain to the defence as well) and when moving, and that while in attacking they present an ever-shifting mark to the enemy, they fire at a fixed object. The latter, however, is weighted with the drawback that the mode of advance is by 60 yard rushes, under the load of a knapsack,‡ and that the range is constantly changing. §

Lastly. The assailant has the great moral advantage of leaving the dead and wounded behind, and has the excitement of the forward movement, which, being in individual order, can be made more quickly, and is not now so hampered by obstacles.

ADVANTAGES OF THE DEFENSIVE.

Let us now consider the advantages of the defensive, particularly with reference to the tactics of to-day. With the new arms, its fire has gained considerably in range, rapidity, and accuracy, and with small-arms in grazing effect.‖ When these advantages can be brought fully into play, the assailant is now forced to cross a widely increased fire zone, where the intensity of fire is also greater than of old. The defender in the meantime is firing at rest from a rest, more or less under cover, at ranges more or less foreknown, and with supports and reserves under cover and closer at hand; and also, except when taking the offensive, he feels, much less than the assailant, the greatly increased difficulty of controlling troops once launched into action.

From the nature of the case, particularly when railway transport is available, and time and distance justify its use, the defence is generally well situated as regards supplies and tools, and in the power of its artillery, being able to bring the heavier natures into action, as was done by the French at Orleans, and by the Germans on the Lisaine, in 1870-71. For the same reason, the question of reserve ammunition is one that can be arranged beforehand by the defence, and is a great difficulty for the attack.

Increased Facilities for Counterstroke.

Although in acting offensively, the defender subjects himself to many of the disadvantages to which an assailant is exposed, still the defensive preparations of the latter cannot be extensive, and several causes now combine to aid the offensive character of the defensive. The great retaining power of the breech-loader enables comparatively few men to hold the defensive zone, thus freeing large numbers for offensive action, and the rapidity of the defender's fire makes it less necessary for him to use obstacles simply to gain time to fire on the attack:

* Hoffbower mentions, that while in action with his battery at Coulombay, he only twice got a glimpse of guns, &c., on which to direct his aim; the smoke and flash being generally the only mark.—" The German Artillery in the battles near Metz ;" translated by Hollist.

† The hits on deployed infantry at 3,300 and 2,200 yards by artillery fire are put down as 1 to 3.—Home.

‡ In 1870—71 the Germans generally fought in marching order on the offensive, and without knapsacks on the defensive.

§ The introduction of range-finders must be admitted to be a distinct gain to the artillery of the attack. Those in our service have been proved accurate up to 4,000 yards and over.

‖ The former grazing effect, up to 600 yards, of our Martini-Henry bullet has, it is said, been somewhat increased by its reduction to 410 grains.

this frees him from the hindrances to counter-attack, which such obstacles used to cause. Again, the extended order in which alone the assailant can advance, renders him less able to oppose attacks on his flank, particularly from the stage of rapid independent firing to the finish of the assault. Lastly, the flank movements of the defender's reserves are made on interior lines, along prepared communications, over known ground, often also under cover and close up to the front; while flank movements of the attack must more often be carried out at a distance.

Use of Telegraphs, Signals, &c.

The arrangements of the defence generally, and particularly those of the counter attack, are also greatly aided by the use of field telegraphy and signalling to connect the operations, and give the commander an instantaneous knowledge of the state of things.

Change in Defensive Fortification.

The great power and range of musketry fire now render it more efficient for the purposes of close defence than that of artillery, to which a distinct and separate zone of action is more appropriate. The increased power of fire has also led to this change, namely, that while formerly each work or post had mostly to depend upon its own form for musketry flank defence, flanking defence has now become more mutual, one intrenchment being efficiently flanked by another even at ranges of 400 to 500 yards. Hence we have greater simplicity of trace and increased direct fire to the front.

The all-importance of fire has also relatively diminished the value of material impediments, and the fact that the crisis of the fight now occurs *before* the attack closes, has lessened the value of small details of flanking defence, except in restricted areas such as the interiors of villages. At the same time obstacles, when used, are now under effective fire at much longer ranges than formerly.

Above all, the holding of decisive points at considerable intervals apart, is now to a great extent, sufficient to secure the ground between them, if such ground be well flanked and closed, when need be, by obstacles.

Considerations as to the Choice of a Position.

A commander has, therefore, to consider, in choosing a position,*
1st. How to compel the enemy to attack.
2nd. How, when, and where to assume the offensive.
3rd. How, by superiority of fire, to repel and shatter the attack.

The Strategy of the Defensive.

The first is a strategical question, already discussed, as far as space permits.

The Counterstroke.

For the second, as in all cases of offensive action, the answer to the "how" is "strike quick, strike hard, and strike heavy."

To strike "quick," the troops must be formed up near at hand, under cover, and separated from those for the passive defence; they should also be unimpeded in their advance.

To strike "hard," they must, while adhering to the formations of the day, be as much concentrated as possible.

To strike "heavy," they must be the whole of the available force.†

* In addition come the questions of encampment and supply.

† On this subject Scherff holds a position to be a bad one for the offensive-defensive if it require more than half the force for passive defence; and, to be good, two-thirds of the whole force should, he thinks, be available for the offensive. These conditions are often, of course, impossible in covering actions.

B

As to the " when," the defender must be ready to profit by any mistakes made in the conduct of the attack, when, for instance, large gaps are left between the attacking bodies, or when the attack wavers along a part of the front. Yet the whole scheme of the defensive is to take decisive action only when the defensive fire has told to the utmost. This period is, in most cases, arrived at between the approach of the attack to within the most effective musketry range, and the completion of the assault or period of re-action; the more so, as the disorganisation of the attack is then greatest, and its power of resistance, except to its front, is very small; even cavalry flank attacks being then, it is thought, practicable for the defensive. An earlier advance on the part of the defender subjects him also to the disadvantages of the assailant, particularly as his formation will be somewhat dense. Success, too, will be less likely if the assailant, when repulsed, can fall back on cover of any kind and assume the defensive.

The decision as to the " where," must be arrived at by the commander according to the situation, and must be thought of in preparing the position. Assuming that one flank at least is secured from a turning movement, the counterstroke may probably be best made from the other, where, if the troops be massed in echelon, under cover, they will also be at hand to resist any turning movements. Occasionally the advance may be made from between two decisive points, the ground between which has been kept clear for the purpose, after which the troops, by turning right or left, may take the attack in flank. This has, however, the great disadvantage of masking the fire of part of the defensive zone.*

With a view, therefore, to the offensive, the position should have sufficient depth for manoeuvring, and one or both flanks secured. It should have free lateral communications, hidden, if possible, from the front. It should provide cover behind woods, undulations, &c., for the concealment where wanted, of large bodies of troops. It should not, by its formation to the front, impede the counterattack or aid the assailant in taking the defensive.

The Passive Defence.

For the passive defence, the position is good chiefly in so far as it favours fire-action and provides cover.† Hence it should afford the following advantages :—

1st. A clear field for fire, with cover and room for the defenders.
2nd. Security for the flanks.
3rd. Strong decisive points in the line.
4th. Strong defensive positions for the reserves, and to cover retreat.
5th. Free communication both lateral and to the rear.
6th. Obstacles in front under fire, and which do not hinder counter-attack.

Clear Field for Fire.

The first and all-important point is to have the widest possible space to the front exposed to fire; if possible, up to the extreme range of artillery, but at all events up to the limit of effective musketry fire.

The causes that affect this are—

    (1) The form of the ground.   (2) Surface obstructions.

On a level plain the least obstruction gives cover; thus, even a line of skirmishers partly conceals its own supports. Hence, as the assailant has to get what cover he can, while the defender can generally use artificial means; a level country, particularly when much enclosed, is the least favourable for defence.‡

* The Duke of Wurtemberg ascribes the failure of the French counter-attacks to their exclusive use of the direct offensive.

† A salient defensive zone has the advantage of inviting or compelling attack.— WAGNER (Grundriss der Fortification).

‡ This is particularly the case in England. We are fortunate, however, in having between the capital and the south coast, at least one range of heights, with, in general, a clear foreground and good command.

Ground falling gently from the position both gives the defender the power of seeing all the foreground, and protects his works from being seen into. For artillery fire, a fall of 1 in 100 is said to be most favourable, while in our service the limit of depression is about 5 deg.* Even for infantry, a steep slope to the front is not desirable, as it is more difficult to fire down it, and men are more exposed in doing so. (Fig. 23, Plate VI.)† Even a comparatively gentle slope of 5 deg., if it extend for some hundred yards, is a severe check to a rapid advance, while on slopes of 10 deg. and upwards, a rush for any distance is impossible.

The position may be
(1). On a slope rising to the rear.
(2). On one rising to a plateau which may have reverse slopes.
(3). On a hog's back or narrow ridge.

In the first case, the defender may secure the advantage of tiers of fire, the guns being posted on high ground behind the infantry‡; the ground, too, diminishes the grazing effect of the assailant's fire. At the same time there is often a difficulty in concealing movements and screening the reserves, and, in case of retreat, the troops are for some time exposed, though the rear guard can generally be well posted to cover the movement.

In defending a plateau, the most favourable position is the forward brow; advanced terraces and knolls, which favour distant fire, being sometimes occupied by the guns and infantry told off to begin the fight. The salient spurs of the brow are the best infantry positions, while guns are often well placed in the re-entering bends or, when the plateau has a gentle rise, on higher ground in rear of the brow. If the brow be straight and the plateau level, the guns may be on the brow, and the infantry positions some way down the slope. When, owing to steepness or obstructions, the forward slope is unfavourable, and the plateau is wide and clear, it may be best to use it as a foreground; but, in any case, the position should be well in front of the rear brow: § for, in case of retreat from a position on that brow, the assailant at once seizes commanding ground from which to fire on the retreating troops, who will suffer in proportion as the slopes are difficult, bare, impeded by obstacles which hinder retreat, such as ravines, marshes, &c., and without defensible localities for the rear guard to hold.

Again, a narrow ridge or hog's back, or a plateau, with a thick wood or other impediment behind it, would not give enough manœuvring depth, and is therefore unsuitable for defence ‖ Ground of the form (Fig. 30, Pl. VI.) would allow the artillery to fire over the first line, and would cover supports and reserves, and also lateral movements.

The reverse slopes should not be parallel to the drop of the projectiles, or they become dangerous for supports and reserves. When so exposed, the steeper they are the better, within the limits suitable for secure and easy movement.

In a position extending for many miles, all forms of ground may have to be dealt

* Captain Hime, R.A., (prize essay). Brunner, however, ("Leitfaden zum unterrichte in der Feldbefestigung") gives the limit of depression as 7 to 8 deg. for guns, and 45 deg. for infantry. Artillery can, of course, defend much steeper slopes by being posted so as to fire obliquely down them.

† The German loss in advancing up the long bare slope of 4 deg. or 5 deg. before St. Privat (battle of Gravelotte, 1870) is an example known to every one; while at Spicheren some of the slopes were as steep as 20 deg. (Fig. 23, Pl. VI.)

‡ It is true that in such positions the guns can seldom fire at short ranges on the immediate foreground of the infantry positions in front of them; but they can mutually flank neighbouring foregrounds at ranges such that the trajectory is not too flat. See further on, the defence of Héricourt.—Bethoncourt.

§ Brunner suggests a distance of at least 500 yards from the rear brow.

‖ The depth wanted for manœuvring varies, of course, with the defender's numbers.

with, thus the general line of defence may, in places, be astride a ridge ; in which case the crest should be strongly fortified, and should be most salient, so as to flank the neighbouring parts of the line ; the latter being somewhat retired where they dip into the valleys.*

A line of heights, if not too elevated or steep, may be a good position, as the heights naturally form strong points, commanding the saddle-backs between them, through which an assailant will try to pass : for the same reason, when gaps† occur in a ridge, the shoulders commanding them become of extreme importance.

Obstructions to Fire.

Apart from the form of the ground, vegetation of all kinds, from forests to grass, and in some cases buildings and embankments, are the chief obstructions. The question whether the position can best be cleared of them, or retired from them, must be settled on the spot.

Protection of Flanks.

As a protection against turning movements, one, or if possible, both flanks, should rest on strong, defensive localities, or on rivers, morasses, &c ‡ In the latter cases, these barriers, if impassable, have the serious disadvantage of re-stricting the defender's power of extending to the flank ; while if he can securely hold passages over them, they give him the advantages of defiles, a rapid advance through which, say with cavalry and horse artillery, might enable him to enfilade the assailant's line from his flank, or to frustate a similar attempt on the part of the attack. It was thus that, on the occasion of the sortie of Montretout (1871) five German batteries, posted near Carrière on the right bank of the Seine, en-filaded the French right when attacking the positions of the 5th Army Corps. On the contrary, the danger to the defensive of having woods close up to the front or flank into which the enemy can penetrate, has been shown among other instances at Königgrätz, and on the French left at Spicheren. At the same time it is to be remembered that, when some hundred yards of clear space separate the defender and the border of the wood from which the attack must defile (un-supported by artillery), the advance of the latter ought never to succeed.

Decisive Points.

The localities along the defensive zone should be of the nature of decisive points (with reference to the probable lines of attack), which, by commanding the best lines of approach, of necessity attract the assailant, and between which he cannot venture to pass while held by the defensive. These points should each form an independent command. The defenders are thus so grouped as to be easily kept in hand.

On the offensive zone, these points form pivots for the manœuvring troops, and, if need be, cover their retreat. The part they themselves perform is a purely defensive one, and they should be extensive enough not to be easily sur-rounded ; the spaces between them, to be thoroughly defended by their musketry fire, should not, it is thought, be wider than about 1,000 yards ;§ while the ar-

---

* These parts, which are apt to be seen into, are thus also more easily defiladed. If the outer slope of such a ridge form the flank of a position, it should be thoroughly swept by the fire of its works.

† Those, for instance, at Guildford and Dorking, in the Surrey ridge.

‡ The greatest security is obtained when both flanks are so protected ; thus the lines of Torres-Vedras rested on the Tagus and the Sea, and in the same way, the position of the Germans before Paris (1870-71) between Sevres and Croisay, had both flanks se-cured by the Seine.

§ Brunner recommends that the decisive points be not more than 1,500 paces apart. Wagner, writing in 1872, suggests 800 paces as the widest interval for musketry de-fence.

tillery fire of each will effectively flank the foreground of those next it, even if they be 2,000 yards apart.* It is only, however, when the intervals are thoroughly commanded by musketry that intermediate works can be dispensed with. For wider spaces up to 5,000 or 6,000 yards, if the ground be favourable, the guns at the decisive points will search the whole of the intermediate intervals; but artillery fire *alone* cannot be relied upon to check the advance of skirmishers, and in such cases intermediate posts must be provided; the strength of the decisive points and of the intermediate posts being, as far as possible, proportioned to the intervals between the former.

Again, in order not to require too many defenders, and also with a view to offensive returns, these "forts of the line" should not be too close to each other. On the defensive zone, when the counter attacks are made on a small scale (say with the front of a battalion), clear intervals rather less than one quarter of a mile are required; while on the offensive zone, in order to allow of an advance with the front of a brigade, the intervals should be at least half a mile, and sometimes more.

In the German defensive line south of Paris (1870-71), where it faced the plateau of Villejuif, the villages of Bagneux, Bourg-la-Reine, l'Hay, and Thais, and the park of Chevilly were decisive points, l'Hay being 1,000 yards to the left, and Thais 2,200 yards to the right of Chevilly; while further east the decisive points of the parks of Cœuilly and of Villiers-le-dèsert were about 1,600 yards apart. We shall have occasion, further on, to mention the fight on the Lisaine, where some of the localities were at much wider intervals.

Communications along and to the Rear.

The necessity for the rapid movement of the reserves has already been referred to. Not a little of the labour of preparation often consists in securing this, and the difficulties are increased if the front be intersected by ravines, watercourses, &c.

The communications to the rear should also be considered; the lie of the position being best, if at right angles to them, so as to cover them as much as possible.

Natural Obstacles in Front and Rear.

An impassable marsh or stream in front, and under the fire of the defensive zone, of course hinders the attack: at the same time the obstacle may hamper the defender in taking the offensive.

An obstacle perpendicular to, but ending short of the defender's line, must tend to divide the attack, or else to limit its extent, by confining it to one side of the obstacle.

Again, an impassable obstacle in rear of a position, is fatal in case of a retreat; while, if it be conveniently passable, the holding of the passages gives the defender the advantage of protected defiles.

Occupation of Advanced Posts.

In most cases it will happen that there are localities in front, and occasionally beyond the flanks, which must be occupied or otherwise denied to the enemy. As a rule, the loss of a weak forepost should never be risked, on account of its moral effect, and commonly it will be best to clear away such, or render them useless to the assailant. A strong post, however, (say 500 or 600 yards to the

* With intervals of 1,000 yards between the localities, mitrailleur fire would effectively flank alternate foregrounds; while such fire would command intermediate spaces not exceeding 2,000 or even 3,000 yards in width. The effective range of case from field guns is now less than that of musketry, and shrapnel burst at the muzzle seems to answer as well or better.—Dartmoor, 1875.

front) which can be supported by the musketry fire of the position, if it can be held throughout, will oblige the attack to deploy earlier, will force him to attack it, and while held will take the general line of his advance in flank.

BATTLE OF BELFORT.

Many of the principles referred to are illustrated by the defensive position held against the French before Belfort, in 1871. In the beginning of January, when it seemed certain that Bourbaki, who was behind the Doubs, would try to raise the siege, von Werder moved to his left from Vesoul, in order to fight a covering action between Belfort and Besançon. To gain time for preparation, he checked the French by the action at Villersexel on the 10th, and then fell back towards the fortress which Tresckow was besieging. It was known that Manteufel, with two army corps, was about to move on Vesoul, towards the middle of the month, whence he would act against the French as circumstances required. The problem, therefore, was, how to delay their advance till Manteufel could make himself felt.

A force of about 42,000 men, opposed to an army more than three times its strength, could only attempt this in a position of limited extent, and the dispa-rity in numbers made it important to secure the flanks from turning move-ments. (Pl. I.) Accordingly, the left rested on the neutral frontier at Delle, whence the position ran west to Montbéliard, at the junction of the Lisaine and Allaine. From hence, the left bank of the Lisaine formed the line of defence, the right of which was at Frahir, on the Lure-Belfort road. Beyond this, the Vosges mountains* some 4 or 5 miles to the north, and the difficult nature of the country at their feet, made a wide turning movement round Frahir very difficult.

Nature of Country.

The country west of Belfort is hilly, much cut up by ravines and with many woods, often with thick underwood, and at this time leafless and full of snow, so that while they gave less cover, movement through them was most difficult.†

The main feature of the position was the obstacle in front of the centre, formed by the network of streams below Montbéliard, where the Doubs joins the Allaine and the canal. This drove the assailant either to divide his forces or to fight on a narrow front, while the defender, who held the bridges at Montbéliard and on the Allaine, had complete freedom of action. The obstacle, therefore, played a part not unlike that of the mountain range, which ran towards, and ended short of the outer of the lines of Torres-Vedras.‡

The assailant being between the Ognon and the Doubs, and his inferior ma-nœuvring power being known, it was rightly judged that he would not venture to attack in force on both banks of the latter stream, and as the position, Mont-béliard-Frahir, was astride the great roads Besançon-Belfort and Lure-Belfort, it seemed the more likely battle field, and was prepared accordingly.

The Allaine Position.

In order, as it seems, not to give too great saliency to the centre at Mont-béliard, Debschitz's detachment was intrenched, in the positions indicated, be-tween Croix and Exincourt, with his front partly covered by the elbow of the Doubs and the stream of the Gland ;§ while, were the main attack made south

---

* The passes through the Vosges were broken up by a party of engineers, though the deep snow made this almost unnecessary.

† The woods in front of the Lisaine position were chiefly beech copses of from 5 to 20 years' growth.

‡ Hamley's Art of War.

§ The bridges at Seloncourt and Herimoncourt on the Gland had been blown up.

of the Doubs, he could fall back on the line of the Allaine and the canal.* The bridges across the former at Sochaux, Fesches, Morvilliars, Grandvilliars, Joncherey, and Delle, were ready to be blown up, and 16 siege guns were placed in rear of them to command the passages. The canal itself lies partly in a cutting, and this and the high ground north of the river, afforded good infantry positions, within reach of the reserves behind Montbéliard and Bourogne.

The Lisaine Position.

From its junction with the Allaine, the Lisaine valley is narrow, and has steep ground on each side as far as Héricourt. The stream itself, 15 to 20 feet wide, and 3 or 4 feet deep, is fordable in many places. From Héricourt the valley widens out as far as Chagey, whence the woods shut in the stream and road for more than a mile. Beyond this it again widens out and is marshy, open, and surrounded by woods.

Along the Lisaine position, the decisive points were in most cases at the passages of the obstacle. They were the town and castle of Montbéliard, the village of Bethoncourt, with the railway embankments there and opposite Bussurel, Héricourt, Luze, Chagey, Chenebier, and Frahir, all of which were more or less prepared for defence.† The old citadel, Little Bethoncourt and its churchyard, the fortified hill of Mougnot, and the factory Chevot were held as advanced posts. The village of Bussurel was unoccupied. The high plateau at Moulin Rougeot formed a strong reserve position for the right flank. The infantry positions before the battle and those of the siege guns are shewn on the plan.

Reconnaissances.

While preparing from the 11th to the 15th, the defenders never lost the touch of the enemy, and, till driven in, their infantry outposts were kept some miles to the front—at Arcey and St. Marie for instance. In front of the right flank a reconnaissance was pushed forward to Rouchamps,‡ and a cavalry regiment was sent out on the 14th as far as Luxeuil.

Position of the Reserves.

As a general reserve for the right flank, $6\frac{3}{4}$ battalions and 3 batteries were placed under Keller, north of Brevilliers. Just to the south-east, 2 battalions and 2 batteries were placed as reserves for Héricourt and Bussurel; while by Vieux Charmont, 6 battalions and 4 batteries stood for the support of the Montbéliard section, or, if needed, for Debschitz's detachment.

Advantages and Disadvantages of the Position.

From the above it will be seen that the position, besides being stragetically offensive, had the following advantages, viz. :—
1. An obstacle in front limiting or dividing the attack.
2. A flank secured, and the other partly protected.
3. The front covered by one or more lines of water obstacles.
4. The lines of attack few in number and well defined.
5. In general, good infantry and artillery positions, with clear foreground.
6. The line of the Savoureuse formed a reserve position, on which it was decided to fall back as a last resource.

On the other hand, the position was too extensive for the force; it was much cut up by ravines, and its lateral communications were bad. The right flank was isolated from the right centre; it lacked good artillery positions, and was

* The canal bridges are moveable draw-bridges.
† The buildings and bridges are of limestone.
‡ It consisted of four Cavalry Regiments, one Light Battery, and two Companies of Jagers.—LŒLEIN.—Die operationen des korps des general's von Werder.

too far from the reserves for quick support.   The woods also lay so close to some of the decisive points, that the attack could approach under cover.

The Fight.

On the day of the fight fortune favoured the French ; for, with the thermometer at zero, most of the line of water obstacles along the front was frozen, so as to bear infantry, while guns could cross the morasses.

The general idea of the assailant was * to advance pivoting on the right, which rested on the Doubs, and to attack along the line Montbéliard Chagey.† This was carried out on the 15th, and the French got into Bussurel and accupied the old citadel ; as the latter commanded Montbéliard, the defenders retired to high ground in rear, but held the castle.   The attack failed to carry the advanced posts at Bethoncourt and Mougnot, and was repulsed at all other points.   On the 16th, all attacks on the line Héricourt-Montbéliard were repulsed, but Chenebier was captured, and the German right fell back behind the woods of la Brise and Essoyeux and to Moulin Rougeot.   It now became necessary to make a counterstroke to save the right flank from being turned, and Keller‡ was ordered to take the offensive on the night of the 16th-17th.   He advanced in two columns, occupied Frahir, and got into Chenebier.   The French, however, held on to the upper parts of the latter village, and, after daylight, he had to fall back, but so as to cover the commanding plateau of Genechier and the road to Chagey.   The French, in the meantime, had failed in two night attacks on Héricourt and at Bussurel.

On the 17th attacks against Chagey, Luze, and Montbéliard again failed, and in the night the French, owing to their moral condition, had to retreat.

STRENGTH OF A DEFENSIVE FORCE.

The question as to the least number of troops of the various arms wanted for the defence of a given position, is plainly one dependent on the circumstances of each case, such as the relative strength, numerical or otherwise, of the troops engaged ; the time available for preparation ; the nature of the country, and the capabilities of the position.

Strength of the Infantry.

It has already been noticed that the general idea of the defensive is to occupy the decisive points in force, and only to observe or slightly veil the intermediate spaces ; and again, as all recent experience shows, the defender should aim at repelling the assailant before he closes.   For these reasons, and on account of the terrible loss in retreat under fire, the strength of the defence should be put into the first line.§   It does not, however, appear desirable any longer to use skirmishers two deep under cover, as the loss is probably more than double that with a single line, while the defensive power of the latter is enough for any purpose when the men are as close together as they can be while shooting freely.   For this purpose a pace per man has been found sufficient : ‖ as also the defensive supports can generally be kept close at hand and under cover, they suffer but little in reinforcing, and need not number more than half the strength of the skirmishers.

---

* According to Lecomte (Guerre-Franco-Almande,) " Historique de la première légion le général Cremer and du Rhône."

† A weak detachment was thrown across towards Audincourt, but no serious attack was made on the Allaine position.

‡ With eight battalions, four batteries, and four squadrons.—WENGEN.

§ The main position selected was generally strongly occupied in first line.—BOGUS-LAWSKI.

‖ Scherff, speaking of the passive defence, says, " One skirmisher to every face of front."

while in the case of the immediate reserves, who should also be under cover, a strength not greater than that of the supports, and sometimes as little as $\frac{1}{3}$rd of them, appears to have been found sufficient.* This gives us from 2 to 3 men to the pace for the actual defence of decisive points.

Second and Third Lines.

In addition, in order to give the defensive formation the advantage of depth, whether for support or counterstroke, second and third lines or reserves must be provided, the strength of which should be increased at the most important points, and also in proportion as the interval between the decisive points is greater. If, for instance, the decisive positions occupied $\frac{1}{3}$rd of the defensive line, the strength of these reserves might not be greater than that of the fighting line. This would give us at the lowest from 4 to 6 men to a pace of defended line, or about $1\frac{1}{2}$ to 2 men for each pace of front, of which, however, a proportion may be cavalry. Again, if the keys of the position were to occupy only about 1-6th of the defensive zone, these reserves would probably not be less than three times the strength of the fighting line, making a total of 12 men for a pace of defended line, or two men as before for each pace of the whole line.

Thus, at the battle of Montretout, 19th January, 1871, the Vth German Army Corps mustered about 20,000 men, or about $2\frac{1}{3}$ men for each pace of front, while the assailants, according to Vinoy, were about $10\frac{1}{2}$ men to the pace. With these numbers, the defenders had ample reserves for an offensive return in the afternoon, which drove the French back from the heights of Garches. The position, however, had been fortified for months, and the attacking troops were inferior.

Again, on the Lisaine, von Werder held the position Montbéliard-Frahir with only $1\frac{1}{2}$ men to the pace; and even if it be objected that the defence of the right flank was not successful, and we credit the position Montbéliard-Chagey with the whole of the reserves, we find here that a force of 28,000 men, or barely 2 men to the pace, held a line of 7 miles[†] with complete success, and that too against an army, ill-disciplined and ill-found it is true, but still composed of well armed Frenchmen, and more than three times the defender's strength.[‡]

Strength of Artillery.

Under ordinary circumstances, one cause of the strength of the defensive, lies in the greater opportunities it has for bringing up guns, particularly the heavier natures. As a rule, therefore, the artillery will be in great strength, and the position must be considered with a view to its development. Thus, von Werder on the Lisaine, had about $4\frac{1}{4}$ guns per 1,000 sabres and bayonets. Seeing, however, it is admitted that the assailant can hardly succeed without much previous artillery fire, while after all the main strength of the defensive lies in its infantry fire,[§] it seems reasonable to suppose, in considering the least number, that the artillery requirements of the defensive are rather less than those of the attack; and though it is plainly desirable to be strong in guns, as they are one of the

---

* Scherff and Boguslawski.

† Against this part of the line the French appear to have opposed their 15th, 20th, 24th, and part of their 18th army corps.

‡ In the proposed German scheme for covering Rouen (1870-71) it was intended to have placed strong redoubts for 300 men at a mile apart, and it was thought that under the circumstances, a force of $1\frac{1}{2}$ battalions and 6 guns to the mile could hold the position. In this case the opposing troops were of inferior quality. Brunner, assuming that a weak unfortified position would require 6 men to the pace, considers that a naturally strong position, if unfortified, might be held by 4, and, if fortified, by 3 men to the pace. With the latter Wagner agrees.

§ At Gravelotte, it is said, only 5 per cent. of the German loss was due to the defender's artillery.—Home. With improved fuzes and shrapnel, we may find this per centage somewhat larger in future.

C

factors to be considered in deciding the limit of extension and also the range within which the ground may be flanked between decisive points, still the German proportion of $2\frac{3}{4}$ guns per 1,000 men ought, surely, to be sufficient for a good defence.* In some cases, too, the situation does not present good artillery positions. Thus the position of the Vth German Army Corps already referred to, was so wooded, that only 56 to 63 of the 90 guns of the corps appear to have been engaged on the 19th of January, along a front of nearly four miles ; while south of Paris, where the decisive points stood in bare open plains, a greater preponderance was given to the action of artillery.

Strength of Cavalry.

As regards cavalry, the use of it for preliminary reconnaissances is not less important to the defence than to the attack, and opportunities are now afforded it, while acting as a defensive reserve, for making rapid counter-strokes on dis-organized attacking infantry. Again, great protection is afforded to an exposed flank by pushing large bodies of cavalry many miles outwards to observe the enemy, report his movements, and with the aid of mounted sappers, to break bridges, block roads, and otherwise delay him. Hence the defensive, though it need not be very strong in cavalry, should have enough for the above purposes, according to the more or less favourable nature of the ground †

Strength of Engineers.

On this subject it may at all events be said that the least number cannot be less than that laid down in regulations, namely, one company for each division of 9,400 men, ‡ and when defensive preparations are extensive, there are several reasons why this number will be found too small   In the first place, in order that the commander may rely on unity of plan in his defensive scheme, he makes known his intentions to the officers commanding the artillery and engineers, with whom he consults. To the former, he must look for the defen-sive use of the artillery, while the commanding engineer is naturally charged with the general scheme of fortifying the position. He in his turn will instruct his officers accordingly, and attach them with sappers to the different sections of the defence. The commander of the troops in each section chooses the actual fighting ground, and leaves the supervision of the work of preparing to the engineers of his section   The mass of the work must of course be exe-cuted by the infantry, as with so few sappers, all they can do is to assist their officers to get the work carried out §

Supposing, however, that this supervision can be managed, there is in addi-tion a great deal of work that requires skill and a knowledge of certain trades. In armies raised by conscription, and in those formed as in the American war of

* A British Army Corps, as defined in 1875, has 90 guns to 27,500 sabres and bayo-nets, or about $3\frac{1}{4}$ guns per 1,000, including the reserve artillery—a proportion due to the fact that, with our want of men, we are bound to use artillery as far as possible, to make up for numbers ; the more so as our lack of reserves would be specially felt in replacing technical troops

† At the battle of Belfort, the proportion of cavalry was about one-eighth of the force —Blune, campaign of 1870-71.

‡ In a German Army Corps the "pioneers" are about one-fortieth, while in a British one the sappers are about one-fiftieth of the combatants.

§ Boguslawski, in speaking of the defensive positions before Paris, says —"Possi-bilities and chances should be carefully weighed and the direction of the works should be given to an Engineer officer, under supervision of the officer commanding the sec-tion." At the same time he ascribed a want of unity of plan to the fact that this could not be done in all cases on account of the many other duties, such as bridge and road-making, on which they had to be employed."

1861-64, the proportion of tradesmen, such as carpenters* and masons, is about the same in the ranks as among the civil population, while in this country the majority are retained in the sieve of the labour market; nor do we even secure many navvies or woodsmen in our recruiting net. Hence, much of the timber work and the preparation of walls and barricades, falls to the sapper carpenters and masons. Again, apart from the infantry preparations, the engineers have to direct the making of any batteries required for the guns of position, and the formation of redoubts, &c., for strengthening the flanks, and other important points. In addition to the actual work of fortifying, the clearing of the front must be done by the engineer corps, with the help of infantry working parties. Here again the employment of men accustomed to the use of tools, makes it desirable to work, as far as possible, with sappers; add to which, the corps is charged with all the works of communication and the preparation of field observatories and posts of observation. Under these circumstances, it seems reasonable to believe that for defensive preparations, a much larger force of engineers of all ranks is required.†

PRELIMINARY RECONNAISSANCES.

In the choice of a position, much time may be saved if the ground can be sketched beforehand on a scale of 3 or 4 inches to a mile, the quickest way being to make an enlarged skeleton of the roads, &c., from the route maps (if any exist) on which the slopes and other military features may be clearly laid down. While the ground is being finally reconnoitred, the commander's decisions can then be recorded on the sketch. The reconnaissance should be extended, if possible, to the ground likely to form the artillery positions of the assailant, so as to judge of his probable action, with a view both to the protection and placing of the troops of the defence.

DEFENSIVE FORMATIONS.

While bearing in mind the mechanism of the attack, the defender must regulate his defensive by his tactical arrangements. ‡ Hence, each part should be fit for some tactical unit, from the group that holds a rifle pit, to the battalion that holds a village or an earthwork: hence, too, the whole position should be divided into sections, each of which may coincide with one or several of the decisive points in the line. To each a commander and a given force is assigned. Great care is required to prevent the junctions of contiguous commands from being weak points, and for this reason the sections should be so spaced that a line of probable attack does not fall between them. Thus along the Lisaine front, the division into sections was as follows:—

The first extended from Sochaux to Bussurel, including Montbéliard and Bethoncourt.

The second as far as the graveyard north of Héricourt, thus embracing the great road to Belfort, and including the advanced post of Mougnot.

The third as far as Chagey, including Luze.

The fourth included Chenebier and Frahir.§

* Some of the regiments of the North in the late American war were almost all backwoodsmen.

† The arrangements for the field telegraph, it is assumed, would be carried out by the half telegraph troop with each Army Corps.

‡ "Instead of making the fight dependent on the intrenchments, we would make the intrenchments dependent on the fight"—*Tactical retrospect.*

§ The following were the forces in fighting line for each of these sections, exclusive of the guns of position :—

For the first,	8 battalions	2 squadrons and	2 field batteries		
For the second,	7 "	2 "	4 "		
For the third,	6 "	4 "	5 "		
For the fourth,	3 "	2 "	3 "	—WENGEN.

Infantry Dispositions.

The front of a position at the decisive points is held by a thick chain of skirmishers with their supports in small bodies close in rear of them, behind these come the immediate reserves. Thus, on open ground, with a battalion of eight companies, each 120 strong, each company might throw forward a half company, extending 40 men as skirmishers and 20 as supports, 80 or 100 yards in rear, while the remaining half companies would be posted some hundred * yards further back, often behind the flanks of the post, and covered, if need be, by intrenchments.

While the shooting line, reinforced by the supports, opposes its fire to the assailant's advance, opportunities will occur for the *reserves* to strike at him as he closes or after his entry. This distinction is important, because the opinion is often held that the defensive arrangements at every point should admit of a direct advance of the shooting line. Such is not the impression given by the German defensive works of 1870-71. the shooting line along the decisive points was generally solidly covered, and was meant to stick to shooting, while passages for counter attack were provided either by the clear spaces between the main defences, or, if these spaces had been closed with obstacles, by allowing the lines of defence to over-lap, so as to permit of offensive returns, the performance of which fell, more often, when on a small scale, to the immediate reserves, while, on a large scale, they were carried out by other troops, namely, those of the second and third lines. These were placed out of fire, but as close to the front as they could be †

Infantry Fire Tactics.

The shooting line generally reserves its fire for the most effective ranges, but in conjunction with the guns pushed forward to force on the development of the attack, small infantry parties will be employed to fire at long ranges, either on bodies of troops when visible, or so as to search out hollows and undulations of ground, &c.,‡ the directions of which should be previously marked and their distances found out.

Second and Third Defensive Lines.

It will occasionally happen that second and even third defensive lines may be provided by intrenchments in rear of the first line. Thus, before Paris, the 10th German division occupied two sections, each about 1,500 yards along the first line. At 1,100 yards in rear there was a second position on the plateau of La Celle St. Cloud, and 700 to 1,300 yards in rear of the second was a third from Le Butard to Bougival.

The Artillery Positions.

To the question, "what to fire at ?" § the only safe answer seems to be " guns should bear on that arm that threatens most" ‖, and this, at first, will often be the attacking artillery. still, it seems agreed that the main duty of the defender's guns is to fire on any bodies of attacking infantry which can be reached. Occa-

---

* Scherff recommends a distance of 300 or 400 paces from the skirmishers, so as to put them somewhat beyond the effect of artillery fire aimed at the latter

† Before Paris, each division was given its own defensive zone, which it occupied with a brigade and artillery. The rest of the division formed a second line in support, while the remainder of the army corps formed a third line or general reserve.—BOGUS-LAWSKI.

‡ The Martini Henri rifle, with the reduced bullet of 410 grs, ranges 2000 and 1500 yards, with elevations of 7¾ deg and 5¼ deg, and the drop at these ranges is about 1 in 6 and 1 in 8. while at 100 and 500 yards, it is only about 1 in 15 and 1 in 40.

§ See Capt. Hime's, R.A. prize essay of 1872.

‖ Hamley.

sionally, as the assailants' guns wheel for action, they should be fired upon, but, as a rule, the maxim of Prince Hohenlohe will be followed, viz., "Never fire at the enemy's artillery when there are any other troops to fire at." *

The defender's artillery should, like that of the attack, be able to take part in the fight from first to last. While, however, the attacking guns take ground to the front once or twice, those of the defender generally remain stationary, and, protected by pits and batteries, fire at the last on the assaulting infantry at short ranges. As the crisis of the musketry fight takes place some 300 or 400 paces in front of the defender's shooting line, it is desirable that the guns be then as much retired as is permissible, bearing in mind the preliminary stages of the attack, for were they very far back, the zone of their fire would be much limited. As a mean between the two, some of the guns will be placed in line with the immediate reserves about 400 paces behind the shooting line, where they do not offer a double mark. Here they cannot, it is true, use the direct fire of case, but they can still join in, right or left, with shrapnel; while were they in the shooting line, exposed to the fire of both arms directed on it, many of them would probably be silenced just when most wanted. Even if the shooting line be carried, guns, as far back as the reserves, can then fire with case to check the assailant's further advance.

With salient decisive points, the guns can be retired between them so as to flank the approaches.† Thus between Chevilly and Thais, south of Paris (1870-71), the artillery positions were well retired, 24 guns being placed in pits along the great road from Choisey, where it crosses the route d'Antibes at la Belle Epine.

Choice of Ground for Guns.

In choosing ground for his guns, the defender has to see—
(1) That they can be got into position without great difficulty.‡
(2) That the position favours direct fire on the distant foreground.
(3) That it permits of a concentrated fire on the lines of approach.
(4) That it allows of a cross fire on the infantry as they close.
(5) That it is secure from enfilade fire,§ and hard to assault.

As to the first, our guns and gunners will always go wherever guns can go; but time and labour are saved if they can be got easily into place.

Few positions will at the same time fulfil all these conditions. In some cases, as for instance when opposing a landing, artillery may be screened on a flank by the form of the ground. (Fig. 40, pl. vii.)

In using the flanking fire of guns, it is to be remembered that splinters from field shells range 400 or 500 yards, and may strike the defenders when not well covered. With case shot also, which is used up to 200 yards, the spread is so great ‖ that the guns cannot safely fire along the borders of the defensive zone.

* Artillery is said, by the same authority, to have been decisive against artillery at ranges not exceeding 2000 paces in 1870-71. If shrapnel can be at all as well timed in war as at practice, this, as regards the men and teams, will now probably be increased to 3000 paces.

† The heavier natures being the least easily moved, are generally those placed further to the rear.

‡ On the Lisaine, roads had to be made in order to get up some of the guns, and even then, many had to be moved by hand.

§ When the assailant's guns become masked by his infantry, he will probably turn them on the guns of the defence, which at that stage are wanted specially to fire at the attacking infantry.

‖ The cone of dispersion of case is often as much as 10° from the gun up to 200 yards; beyond this it is very uncertain. With shrapnel the dispersion is 6° or 7° from the burst.

In general, the flanks of a position should be strong in artillery, both as a protection against turning movements, and to hinder the assailant from placing batteries to enfilade the defensive line, * but some of it may be drawn, when wanted, from the reserves.

German Artillery Positions, Battle of Belfort.

The following sketch of where the guns stood along the Lisaine,† will help to explain much that has been referred to .—

To begin at Montbéliard, on the morning of the 15th, a field battery stood at the old citadel, and another by the town. In the castle, which was prepared as a keep, were two 12-prs and four heavy 6-prs ; the latter fired on the citadel and along the road to Arcey On the hill of la Grange Dame, five long 24-prs. were placed in a sunken battery, so as to fire down the gentle slope towards the town, and also so as to command the opposite heights and the valley to the north almost up to Bussurel.

At Héricourt, a light battery fought, at first, in gun-pits at Mougnot, and was afterwards intrenched on the hill of Salamon at the railway station, near which were two other batteries in gun-pits. These could all fire down the valley and sweep the passages at Bussurel, they also commanded the plateau of Tavey and the great road to Belfort. This plateau and road were further commanded by seven 12-prs. intrenched on high ground north of Héricourt ; while between that town and Luze there were 30 field guns in gun-pits‡ dug out of the lower slopes of Mont Vandois. Some of these fired up to Chagey , while the mass of them commanded the valley and open ground by Couthenans and the road Béverne-Héricourt. For the defence of Chenebier, two batteries were placed north of Bas-des-Essert , while three 24-prs § stood at Moulin Rougeot, and could fire to Frahir and Evette ‖

Considerations as to Ground.

As to the ground, favourable slopes should be sought, as well as accidents or undulations, which can be easily turned to account for cover for guns and their limbers close at hand. The nature of the soil, too, as affecting both the making of cover and the bursting of the enemy's shells is to be considered. Hard, rocky, or stony ground is in both ways bad, and increases the effect of splinters, &c

* Even the unaimed infantry fire of a flank attack seriously affects the defender.

† Along the Allaine the guns of position stood as follows, viz —
Two 6 prs N W. of Sochaux, firing to Exincourt , two 6 prs by Allanjoie, command-ing Fesches.
Two 24-prs to E and two to W of Bourogne, commanding the passages of the St. Nicholas stream and the road to the bridge of Morvilliars
Two 12-prs. behind Grandvilliars , four 24-prs behind Joncherey ; two 12-prs E. of Delle
The German 6, 12, and 24-prs throw shells of about 14, 30, and 56 lb respectively.

‡ With the exception of four in a hollow road and two behind a hedge

§ These were got up by hand from before Belfort, when the flank was threatened — LŒLEIN.

‖ In the fire contest on the 16th of January, the flanking power of modern firearms was well shewn. The French, after failing to cross the Lisaine from Bussurel, attacked both at Héricourt and Bethoncourt As they did so, the three German batteries, which had supported the fight on ground N.E of Bussurel, turned their fire across the front of Mougnot , while the left company behind the railway embankment before Bussurel fired on the assailants across the front of Bethoncourt As the French skirmishers dipped into the valley their supports, debouching from the Bois Bourjois, fired over their heads , while the Germans at Bethoncourt replied with tiers of musketry fire At the same time, two batteries to the S E of Bethoncourt joined in the fight while the guns on la Grange Dame brought a flanking fire to bear on the assailants The attack was repulsed and renewed, and, on this occasion, the three German batteries which stood facing Bussurel, fired down the valley in support of Bethoncourt,

Artillery Fire Tactics.

The mass of the defender's guns will not generally open except at effective ranges; but to force the assailant to deploy early, detachments of horse artillery and cavalry, and sometimes small infantry parties, are posted forward for a time, and are afterwards rapidly retired, so as not to mask the fire of the position. These advanced parties should be far enough forward to check the assailant under fire of the defender's guns, but beyond the range at which he could use musketry against the guns.

Reserve Artillery.

A proportion of guns must be kept with the other arms in reserve, either to reinforce threatened points, or to accompany a counter-stroke. Of the 130 field guns available along the Lisaine, 34 were in reserve, or (including the position guns), rather more than one-third of the whole.*

Mitrailleurs.

Guns of this class represent the fire of a certain number of infantry, in a small space, with a somewhat greater effective range than the latter. Their fire has none of the searching and destructive power of common shells, and they should not be pitted against artillery. They are also more dependent on a knowledge of the range, which the latter can judge by its effects.† It seems to be thought that the use of these guns will be confined to the defensive; still, owing to their mobility, a defender may occasionally employ them to accompany the offensive action of horse artillery, either in the development of the fight before the assailant's guns are in a position to crush them, or with flanking parties to aid them in checking the advance of flank attacks along roads, or as they debouch from woods or defiles. Their chief use, however, will be to fire at critical moments, on restricted areas, and in definite lines, as on bridges,‡ down streets, &c., and also for the close flanking defence of decisive points, where, the dispersion being more regulated, they are safer than guns firing shells or case. In the latter positions they may often be screened from the direct fire of artillery and may fire through loopholes in walls. In all cases they should be concealed so as to act as a surprise §

PREPARATIONS FOR DEFENCE.

The position being decided on, the first consideration is the amount of time available. It may be foreseen that the work can be spread over many weeks; or, again, from the known position of the enemy, several days may be counted on, as was the case on the Lisaine. It often happens, however, when in the pre-

* Of these, three batteries were brought up in support at Bussurel, and four batteries afterwards accompanied Keller's counter-attack.

† The service Gatling (bore 0·45 ins., weight complete 16¼ cwt.) fires 400 rounds a minute, the greatest effect being up to 1200 yards. Repeated trials at Shoeburyness, at ranges of from 300 to 1200 yards, showed that one Gatling represents the fire of about 22 infantry with Martini-Henri breech-loaders, and for these ranges makes nearly as many hits as would be made by two 9-pr. muzzle loading rifle guns. It has the power of dispersion, there is no recoil, and, unlike the French gun, its fire is continuous, and does not attract much attention by its noise. Each gun has 2,400 rounds, with a reserve of 3,600, *but does not fire small arm ammunition.* It is sighted to 2,400 yards (elevation 8·22.) On this subject see a paper by Captain Owen, R.A., in Vol. VIII. Royal Artillery Institution Papers.

‡ Several cases are recorded, in 1870-71, at Gravelotte, Sédan, and elsewhere, in which the Germans, in debouching from cover within range of mitrailleurs, suffered very severely from their fire: for instance, Lœlein mentions that the Germans, in attempting to retake Chenebier, lost 21 men by a single discharge from a mitrailleur; the French having brought in several of them for the defence of the place.

§ Gatling guns being without recoil, may be used with ease in towers or rooms, or in small boats, caponiers, blockhouses &c.

sence of the enemy, that he will attack on the morning after his approach, or even on the day itself. If the former, a night is available for preparing   Even in the latter case, an army corps, with two roads for its advance, occupies nine miles in length, and requires several hours after the advanced guards are engaged for the complete development of its attack.* Hence, though the contingency seems hardly to apply to the case of a position *selected* as a field of battle, yet, even under these circumstances, troops may prepare under cover of skirmishers till almost under fire , † the real difficulty being, not so much the want of time to do the work, as the delay in arranging and getting to work.

Tools and Materials.

Whatever be the time, the amount of work is limited by the tools, &c., available on the spot   The proportion of intrenching to cutting tools should properly vary according to the more or less open nature of the seat of war , but, for the general question of defence, we can only count on the present appliances of our army. Accordingly we find that a section with tools forms part of the Engineer Company with each division, and from the position now assigned to the company in the advanced guard, we may rely on these tools being up when wanted.   With a British army corps there would also be a 4th R.E. company and the tools of the field park ‡

In addition, a tool waggon is now assigned by regulation to each battalion of infantry §   Experience will show whether the regiments will feel the same amount of interest in bringing up these tools as the engineers.   We may, however, assume that each of the 21 battalions of an army corps will now be able to furnish two working companies of 125 men each, with their tools for each relief, viz

For intrenching, 142 , || for sod cutting, 10 ; for clearing timber, &c , 75 , for brickwork, &c , 4 , for reserve, 19   In addition, working parties may be required in proportion to the number of engineer tools available, and also for revetting.   When brushwood has to be cut or used for revetments, some of the work may, if need be, be done with the soldiers' clasp knives

Besides these resources, the officer charged with the defensive preparations will do well, at once, to collect all tools ¶ from the villages, and post sentries over them and any timber or other materials likely to be useful

With the more deliberate operations, or in connection with a siege, the defender may frequently be able to draw on the siege equipment   Thus, the resources of the besieger were also used (1871) in the preparations on the Lisaine.

* The sturdy resistance of the German outposts at Dung and Barth on the morning of the 15th of January, delayed the French attack on Montbéliard till within a few hours of sunset.

† The German Engineers worked at breaking the ice and completing the defences along the Lisaine, after the French advance had sounded —LŒLLIN

A light battery at Mougnot (battle of Belfort) after firing all its ammunition, retired to re-fill, and then intrenched itself *during* the action on the hill of Salamon —WENGEN

‡ Hence the engineer tools, &c , with each company and army corps respectively, may be reckoned as 130 and 606 picks, and as many shovels, 6 and 32 spades, 81 and 495 axes, 13 and 58 hand-saws, 4 and 22 cross cut saws, 40 and 250 bill hooks, 13 and 74 boring and crow bars, 20 and 128 heavy hammers, besides other articles

§ To carry 150 light picks, as many light shovels, 10 spades, 25 felling axes. 50 bill-hooks, and 4 crow-bars.

|| This leaves 8 picks and shovels and 6 axes (pioneers) for use in bivouac.

¶ In an unexhausted district, at least in this country each house of a hamlet would furnish a spade, an axe or hatchet, a bill-hook, a spud or mattock, and a saw , a few wheelbarrows would also be available.

Simplicity in Details.

In the case of hasty operations, works of whatever kind should have the greatest simplicity :—

(1) Of dimensions ; (2) Of arrangement ; (3) In the distribution of labour.

Dimensions and Arrangement of Work.

The dimensions should be few, and in earthworks feet and half-feet are generally the smallest desirable. While adhering to dimensions in the tasks, anything like finish in the form of the parapet is worse than useless.

The work in the field should be simply a reproduction of the peace instructions, modified where need be. Although, in the German defences of 1870-71, there was great variety in the forms of the shelter trenches, yet, in those works which require previous arrangement, they adhered closely to their *reglements ;* these, though not always the best, relieved the officers from having to design, when they were wanted for supervision, and the men from requiring much looking to or explanation.

Distribution and Execution.

In war, where more time is often spent in getting to work than in doing it, and when both time and superintendence may be scanty, simplicity in distribution is of the first necessity. All work should, if possible, be so arranged as to let each man have a distinct task, and, to allow of this, *we* give each digger a pick and shovel. As a rule they should be distributed in a single line at intervals of two paces, closer than which, untrained men cannot work freely. Again, owing to the reducing effects of hardships, and the distances the working parties may have to come, it is well not to calculate on tasks much greater than 80 or 90 cubic feet : though, for spells of an hour only, it is found that men can, at a push, dig out 50 cubic feet from shallow trenches.*

Provided that the depth do not exceed 4 or 5 ft., a digger can manage 80 or 90 cubic feet in from four to six hours, after which little more is to be got out of him : hence, though in siege operations there may often be a difficulty in changing, and longer reliefs, with intervals for rest and food, may be more convenient ; in the field an average of five hours seems best.

Supply and Formation of Working Parties.

In a siege, too, where the work goes on regularly, the infantry working parties are detailed in general orders over night. This, however, is impracticable in more hasty operations, and the officer charged with the defensive arrangements should be in direct communication with the commander of the section, so as, in all cases of pressure, to get the necessary help *without delay.*

As far as possible the company will be the working unit, and will be charged with some one portion of the defences. The superintending R.E. officer or non-commissioned officer should see that all tools he has to supply are ready when wanted, and, in earthwork, that the work is traced beforehand with lines † or pickets, or else *spitlocked* out. ‡

---

* In doing such work, there is not much difference between the small and large tools. In a relief, however, the former do less work, particularly if the task be deep, or the throw long. The large (R.E.) tools should, therefore, be used as far as possible for deep work, and for second and other reliefs. If the small tools must be so used, the men, in day or moonlight, may be only 4 ft. apart ; but, in the dark, all should work at the two pace intervals, and, in heavy work, the parties with small tools may have an extra man for each digger, or two, according to the hardness of the soil ; to keep the tools in use while the diggers rest.

† Each company (R.E.) has twelve hamboro' lines, each 50 yards long.

‡ A supply of stick gauges of the depth and width of the tasks are better than measuring rods.

D

The working columns parade under their own officers, and with the tools of their own battalion, as far as they go * There should be, with each, a reserve of, say, 10 men per cent.†

Employment of Civilian Labour.

When preparation is made at leisure, the civil population may sometimes be induced or forced to help, but, without military organisation, the results are not always satisfactory‡ still, owing to the pressure of war, work by contract may be unavoidable, and the best safeguards are to have every detail decided on in peace, and so designed that the work may be capable of defence at each stage ; and to employ reliable men to execute it

In countries where Europeans can work but little, native corps are organized by the Engineers, as was done most successfully in the war of 1874, in Ashantee.

CLASSIFICATION OF DEFENSIVE WORKS.

In the preparation of a position the work to be done consists of—§
(1.) Clearing the foreground for fire.
(2.) Covering the shooting line.
(3.) Covering the guns
(4) Covering the supports and reserves.
(5.) Placing obstacles.
(6) Making communications.
(7.) Laying field telegraphs, putting up field observatories and signal stations, measuring and marking out ranges.
(8.) Preparing rear-guard stand-points

CLEARING THE FOREGROUND.

(1.) The importance of denying cover to the assailant has now become so great, that the work of clearing the front and flanks must be undertaken systematically In each class of work, a proportion of the cutting tools with the Royal Engineers and the regiments will be required, and circumstances must decide the number available for clearing, and consequently the strength of the parties. Timber of all sorts is that which most often screens the advance ; hedges, even when perpendicular to the front, now impede lateral movements less, while they act as screens from the defensive cross-fire ; wire fences, however, are kept as obstacles

Clearing Timber.

The time required for clearing is always rather uncertain ‖ In clearing woods,

* They also generally parade with arms, and always with filled water bottles

† Some of the reserve do odd jobs , others replace casualties, or help men to finish, who are unavoidably behindhand. If, through neglect, men do not finish they should be kept back till they do , in the case of another relief, helping those who are set to their unfinished work

‡ Vinoy in the " Siège de Paris," complains bitterly of the way in which the first preparations were spun out by the contractors and their labourers.

§ The works connected with encampments, water-supply, &c , must also be provided for

‖ The following results may give an idea of the time Hedges have been cut down by men at two pace intervals, in from 6 to 18 minutes , if very bushy, a pole and ropes may be used to expose the lower branches to the axe (Fig 16, pl V) Troops, at 5 paces apart, clear 30 paces forward in brushwood five or six years old in 8 hours Again, in felling hop woods of ten years growth, a woodman, in this country, clears 5 paces by 36 paces in a day Two untrained soldiers, with axes, cut down trees of 4, 6, 9, 12, and 18 inches in diameter in about 1 3, 5, 9, and 15 minutes respectively. Soft wood trees (when not more than two to three feet in diameter) can be felled in 20 to 30 minutes by 4 men , if of hard wood they may take three times as long Large trees when felled must often be lopped so as to prevent them acting as cover on the ground

the men are commonly at five pace intervals. Bill-hooks are the best tools for brushwood; axes for small trees; while, with cross-cut saws for those over 9 in. in diameter, the work is done in about half the time required with axes. Gun-cotton can rarely be spared to cut down trees. Used as necklaces, it is not reliable, and about ten times as much of it is required as when augur-holes are used. The power of cutting down trees instantly, may be valuable when it is wanted to unmask a battery, or unexpectedly to barricade a road or passage, which may thus be kept open to the last moment.

Occasionally, tall grass, corn, or reeds may impede the defender's fire, and should be trampled down by men in line, or cut down, or burnt.*

Timber felled in clearing, has often also to be moved for defensive use. The wagons of the Pontoon Train, when available, are convenient for carrying small trees and brushwood, but for heavy logs, *devil-carts* are best.

The wagons of the Engineer Train with an Army Corps carry some spare wheels and axles, and others are often to be got from country carts, &c. Poles, (fig. 17, pl v.) can be fixed to these axles in an hour or two, and the spare drag-chains used as slings. The working parties can then handle the timber with ease, aided by troop horses with lassoes.

Clearing away Walls and Filling Hollows.

Walls, unless very thick, can be knocked down by from 15 to 20 men using a trunk of a tree, or a railway bar, as a ram; this saves gun-cotton. Low buildings may be similarly treated; if high, they must generally be blown down.† The ruins must be levelled so as not to give cover.

Hollows are best filled with abatis; they may sometimes be inundated.

Where to Clear.

Cover should be removed wherever it is judged that the assailant can make most use of it.‡ Slopes swept by the defensive fire should be cleared in preference to those which lie facing the position, and can be better seen into, and through which an advance may be impeded, even by narrow belts of entanglements. Again, it is most important to clear away, in front of localities occupied as decisive points, any enclosures or other cover extending beyond the limits of the shooting line. Every effort should be made to clear from the front to a distance of from 400 to 600 yards, particularly on those portions of ground, where the attacking skirmishers will make their stand for the fire contest with the defenders. In a very open country, the clearing may occasionally be carried much further forward. The clearing parties are also charged with the destruction or barricading of advanced communications, fords, and bridges. These works should be carried out up to the limit of the defensive fire, and further, if likely to cause much delay. On a line of river obstacle, the bridges§ may be blown up, prepared for demolition, or only barricaded. Thus, to return to our example, the

* At Wissemberg, in 1870, the French fire from the hill of the Geisberg was thus impeded.

† Each R.E. company carries 500 lbs. of gun-cotton. A pound to a foot cuts down an 18-in. wall when laid untamped on the ground against it; while less will answer if well tamped.

‡ Trees on the defensive line and in rear often screen without hindering the defenders, and should be left, when they do not give a mark to fire at; single trees, too, may be left in front to mark ranges. Trees should be felled so as to lie, "tips to the front," as otherwise even their trunks may give the assailant cover, and also they are more easily passed.

§ Stone bridges can hardly be destroyed without explosives, neither can large girders. The gun cotton should therefore be chiefly saved for these. Small girders can be thrown off their bearings, and wooden bridges can, if need be, be cut down, or, which is less certain, burnt with petroleum.

road bridges over the Allaine were all mined, and the railway bridges destroyed. A bridge at Montbéliard, one at Bethoncourt, and two at Bussurel were blown up, that at Hericourt was mined, but kept open, on account of the forepost at Mougnot, while the bridge at Luze was only barricaded, as the ice above it bore infantry, and, as in the case of a neighbouring ford or passage, nothing would have been gained by destroying it.

COVER FOR DEFENCE.

We have already seen that the chief defensive preparations are to be made along the fronts of the decisive points, and above all at the flank or flanks exposed to turning movements, and here they should be begun earliest

The moral effect of cover is to give confidence to the defender and to discourage the assailant, particularly when he only learns its strength as he closes to attack.

The material effects are, to diminish the loss and conceal the effects due to fire, and also to conceal the defender's strength and formations. The advantages of cover are self-evident, but their extent is perhaps best realized by looking at the results of recent *successful** defensive actions   Bogulawski gives the average loss of the Germans, on the defensive, as 1 15th or 1-16th; while he mentions that the losses of those of their troops actually engaged at Gravelotte were almost 1-4th.   He estimates their loss at the battle of Montretout at 750, (1-29th†) while the French lost 3,000 to 6,000 men ‡   Again, on the Lisaine Werder's loss was about 1780 men (1-24th§), while he inflicted a loss of 5,000 or 6,000 men on the assailant.   Such results speak for themselves,|| as to the power both of avoiding and inflicting loss that preparation gives the defender   In providing cover, we have to remember that war, being wasteful alike of life and labour, demands quantity more than quality in the work to be done . hence we should not aim at impossible perfection, and thereby cramp its extent ; the total loss being most diminished by giving the best cover we can to the many, rather than perfect cover to the few ; for however imperfect cover may be, it will always diminish the per centage of loss, and even a mistaken sense of security makes men shoot straighter than without it ¶

COVERING THE SHOOTING LINE.

Cover for the shooting line consists —

1st, of prepared localities, such as villages and enclosures, with their hedges, banks, and walls , of forests, woods, &c , and of portions of railroads.

2nd, of shelter trenches and epaulments.

3rd, of redoubts.

* In defeat, on the contrary, that "Mors et fugacem persequitur virum ' is now more than ever true

† 650, RUSTOW (war for the Rhine frontier).

‡ 3,000, VINOY

§ According to Lohlein and Wengen   about 1-3rd of these fell in the fighting round Chénebier   Lohlein gives the French loss as 8,000 to 10,000

|| Maurice, in his Wellington essay, mentions that the French losses, on the defensive, were only ½, while on the offensive they were 3½rd times those they caused the Germans

¶ It should be remembered that blind field shells, such as those of our 12 pr B L R , only penetrate 3 or 4 feet into earth at 1,000 yards' range , 2 feet or less into brickwork , 1 foot into rubble masonry , and 2 feet into solid oak   the penetration of the live shells being less   While at the shortest ranges the 480 gr M H bullet, perhaps the heaviest of the new musket bullets, will not penetrate more than 12 or 13 inches into loose and 10 or 11 inches into rammed earth or sand bags , nor will it pass through soft wood logs of 10 inches, or hard logs of 5 inches diameter, nor through 3-8th inch iron or 3-16th inch steel plates , and these penetrations are generally much greater than those of shrapnel bullets and of small splinters.   With shrapnel at Dartmoor (1875), many bullets, no doubt after graze, stuck in the ¾ inch fir of the targets.

All these means of defence are combined with obstacles and worked in together, so as to enclose the decisive point with a continuous line. There is a maxim more preached than practised, namely, that infantry must never be put behind walls exposed to artillery. If exceptions are wanted to prove the rule, the late war furnishes plenty. It is doubtless wise not to put men behind walls if you can do better, but the fact is, the effects of artillery on walls are much over-rated.[*] It is to be remembered that what gives cover from musketry fire, protects also from most of the effects of artillery: for of the small proportion of casualties caused by shells, nearly all are due to the effects of shrapnel or splinters, both of which are completely stopped by walls, while a field shell on striking a thin wall, makes a hole of $1\frac{1}{2}$ to 2 feet, bursting only if used with a percussion fuze, and then with small lateral effect.[†] Upon buildings, the effects are more serious in proportion to their height, and a concentrated fire will render them untenable, but will rarely make them unfit for occupation when it has ceased. We see, therefore, that villages and enclosures give good cover, and conceal the positions of supports and reserves: hence they have played, and continue to play, a part in tactics, increasing in importance in proportion to the development of skirmishing, and to the decrease of cavalry action on the battle field.[‡]

The position of villages is often very important, lying as they sometimes do astride rivers, or on ridges commanding roads, as is the case of many round Metz.

Uses of Localities.

In the defence of a position, villages, farms, and enclosures may be used occasionally as *detached posts*, frequently as *posts of observation* and *advanced posts*, and constantly as decisive points in the shooting line, or as réduits for reserves. In any case the houses shelter the troops.

Detached Posts and Posts of Observation.

For a detached post, a strong building or group of houses is chosen and prepared according to the rules in books, every obstruction being cleared away all round for some hundreds of yards if possible. They are chiefly used where not much exposed to artillery; often to check the turning of a flank.

Posts of observation must often be abandoned, but their use may be denied to the enemy by choosing the building which will make[§] the biggest shell, lodging charges in it (under earth if exposed to guns) and firing them by fuze or electricity: or the buildings may be prepared for burning[||] Gas too, it is thought, may supply a ready means for extensive demolitions by regulating its escape and

---

[*] Vinoy mentions that in attacking the German positions south of Paris from l'Hay to Choisy, the right attack failed because the German infantry held a wall at the former place under the fire of 25-prs. from Les Hautes Bruyères, distant only 1,200 yards. Again, the sortie of the Imperial Guard from Metz, by Ladonchamps (1870), which was preceeded by a heavy cannonade, was for a time completely checked at St. Remy, by two landwehr battalions behind a wall which a horse could jump.

[†] Wagner states that an 18 inch brick wall is proof against a German 6-pr. shell at 750 metres: our 16 pr. shell breaks up less readily.

[‡] In the days of Frederic the Great, villages were rather avoided by both sides, and often burnt. More recently we may quote, as instances of fights for localities, those at the village of Vierzenheiligen at Jéna; of Hassenhausen at Awerstaedt; at the brick walls round Lützen; the "Speicher-haus" at Esling; and the farm of Hougoumont, with its 9 ft. wall, at Waterloo.

[§] The Gare-aux-Boeufs, a factory between Vitry and Choisy, was thus used by the Germans in 1870, and on one occasion taken by the French, who however left it in the afternoon, without knowing it was mined. At midnight it was blown to pieces while unoccupied.—VINOY.

[||] Petroleum is now so much used, it can generally be got for burning houses, particularly where there is no gas.

then firing it. Field shells will set fire to buildings, but the fires may be kept under. Bussurel was thus fired in 1871 by the Germans, yet the French stuck to it for three days.

Advanced Posts.

Advanced posts are fortified like others, but, as with redoubts, their gorges should be defensible when surrounded, and yet exposed to the guns of the defence. What answers best, perhaps, when the gorge is not " looked into" from higher ground on the position, is a musket-proof hurdle wall, (fig 2, pl. v) which guns can quickly destroy* : wide exits to retire through are wanted. A most important use of advanced posts is to protect exposed flanks.

Preparation of Villages, &c.

The text books deal with the defensive details of villages and hamlets, but we may notice that the chief innovation is the placing of the shooting line behind advanced enclosures about 50 to 200 paces in front of the houses These enclosures constantly have salient and re-entering portions which furnish flanking defence. Hedges are often inconvenient, but in these cases they come in well, and may be used as screens (figs. 1, 5, and 11, pl v., and 47, pl. vii) or revetments (fig 6, pl v) They are sometimes strong enough to form entanglements when cut down.

Rail fences, like hedges, may be used as revetments for earth, or as supports for log parapets; or they may be planked to act as screens. Walls too, used with earth, act as revetments or as obstacles, or, if in the body of a parapet, as *cores* to burst shells with slow fuzes Sometimes they may be covered by a detached earth screen, (fig. 9, pl. v.) Their chief use, however, is as independent cover for infantry. The books show how they are prepared according to height, thickness, and the command required. If loopholed,† they give most cover, but with only about 40 crowbars to a division, not more than 200 or 300 loopholes can be made in a relief,‡ and these will be in the flanking portions and in the angles of buildings Experience § shows that the quicker methods, viz., using furniture, &c., for banquettes, knocking down the tops of walls (fig 50, pl viii), notching them with a pickaxe, or making log loopholes (fig. 25, pl vi.), are those most often resorted to. For want of sand bags,‖ sods are used to fill up the tops of the notches or build small bonnettes on walls, and also to fill up windows of houses. Dry brick walls may often be built up as breastworks against musketry,¶ and, as we have learned in India, mud walls are quickly made, easily loopholed, and very tough. When high walls are not wanted as screens, the top parts may be knocked down if exposed to guns. A long length of enclosure wall often requires to be traversed with earth or timber (fig. 55, pl viii), and should also be flanked Where the men have to shoot standing in order to see the ground, tambours (figs. 50 and 52,) projecting 10 to 15 feet from the wall may be used if not much exposed to artillery. Sunken caponiers, whenever they are suitable are more easily and quickly made, and are less exposed, (fig. 14, pl v.) Works of this kind, though

* Such a wall has been made in three-quarters of an hour, on a hard road In streets, the earth to fill up with, is carried from the gardens a barrow load fills a pace.

† Loopholes on the ground floor are best made horizontal (4 ins to 6 ins high, and 1 foot wide.) If need be, men can shoot at 2 feet intervals.

‡ The best tools are 18 inch masons' chisels and hammers, with these a man can make a loophole in an 18 inch wall in a quarter of an hour. We carry only 10 to an Army Corps

§ See, further on, the foot note on the defence of Héricourt (1871).

‖ With each division we have 1 000 sand bags A man with a spade cuts 100 sods in an hour Dry bricks can be laid at the rate of one a minute, by each man.

¶ A field shell knocks down a dry stone wall 2 ft. 6 in, thick. Dartmoor, 1875.

rather more roomy, were much used in 1870-71 for advanced positions before Paris, and Boguslawski says they were found to answer best. These works, with somewhat thicker roofs and screened from the front, might also be placed at the shoulders of the shooting line, in front of localities, instead of the small closed redoubts generally recommended, which, by their pretension to strength, are apt to draw a fire that disables them when wanted.

The cover for the shooting line, whatever be its description, should protect the men as much as possible under the preliminary artillery fire, and, when the preparations are not very hasty, a second or even a third defensive zone may be prepared; or the whole village may form a keep: cover for the supports and reserves and cartridge magazines are arranged for; entrances are barricaded, and wide communications, both lateral and to the rear, are provided. The troops for the defence are moved about the village, so as to be familiar with the roads and passages; for the close defence depends, to a great extent, on the prompt action of the supports and reserves. Much depends, too, on the lay of the village; those *end on* to the front (pl iii.) are most liable to enfilade along the main streets, show least front, and want most outworks; but they are least easily turned, and allow of the most protracted defence. If they be very long and straggling, it is sometimes thought best to hold a line of retrenchment across them, and clear as far forward as possible, gutting those houses that are left and bear on the defences. Villages *broadside on* (pl. ii.) show the best front; while compact villages (pl. iv.) answer both purposes. Sometimes positions must be held in rear of villages: these should either be within effective musketry range of the rear outlets, so as to keep in the defenders, as the Germans did at the passages of Bussurel in 1871; or else just within the effective range of guns, so as not to suffer from the covered musketry fire from the village. In general, the supporting artillery is retired on one or both flanks*, as at Héricourt (pl. i.)

Shelter Trenches.

From the sketches (pls. ii. to iv.) it will be seen that earth cover is always more or less used. When either the time for work is very short, or when, as occasionally happens, an advance may have to be made over them, the form (fig. 21, pl. vi.) used by the French and Germans, or our own† field exercise trench may be employed. The former is the least possible obstacle, but though its section is so small, it takes as long to make as the latter, which gives more cover. The lowness of such parapets makes them difficult to hit,‡ but when permissible, better cover should be provided. A shelter trench may be improved§ so as to be available for men firing standing either on the bottom (fig. 20, pl. vi.) or higher up (fig. 23) when required. In intrenching heights, great care is wanted in choosing the exact position on the crest whence the ground in front can be swept. Thus at Spicheren, in 1870, the shelter trenches did not always sweep the slopes before them. The method in fig. 35, pl. vii., may be applied here also.

* Stains was supported by guns on high ground 800 yards to its left rear. Bagneux somewhat the same: while Bourg-la-reine was defended by artillery on the heights of Sceaux. Villages in hollows (fig. 48, pl. viii.) cannot be shelled from a distance.

† Now 4 ft by 1½ ft. The 2 ft. width is too cramped for long use, and in hasty work saves only 12 or 15 minutes.

‡ At Dartmoor (1869), when firing at known ranges up to 1,500 yards on different small trenches, the average of hits on two-deep infantry was four for every ten 12-pr. B.L.R. shells. At 1,200 yards 24 rounds (shrapnell and segment) made 14 hits on 24 ft. of 4 ft. by 1 ft. 3 in. shelter trench containing 15 file of dummies two deep. Again, in 1875, 48 9-pr. M.L.R. shells (common, water and shrapnel) fired to enfilade a 2 ft. by 1 ft. 6 in. trench, at angles with its crest of 33° and 19°, and at known ranges of 1,455 and 1,930 yards, made 29 hits on 46 dummies, 4 ft. high and one pace apart.

§ The deeper trenches have, of course, the disadvantage of giving more cover to a successful assailant.

When a relief is available, cover can be provided, in which the shooting line can crouch down at moments of great exposure The sections (figs 25 and 29), are sufficient for most purposes, and these, or the smaller kinds, might be used according to the situation, the time, and the tools available In all of them, great protection is afforded if board-troughs, brushwood-cylinders (fig. 19), or logs of wood can be used to form loopholes Occasionally very exposed portions of the line may be blinded somewhat as in fig 14, pl. v.

If the position be in a very open country, shelter trenches and breastworks, with perhaps a few redoubts, will form the bulk of the defences.

Trench-Work by an English Division

We have seen that with each division* we may expect to have about 130 engineer, and 1,000 infantry sets of picks and shovels ; and a division, having to intrench itself in first line, could generally be reinforced by half of the 4th Royal Engineer company with the corps. This would make up the tools in round numbers to 1200 sets † These, with only a clear half or three quarters of an hour for work, would give the power of making 2,400 paces of common shelter trench, or of section 21. With about an hour available, we could throw up about 1,800 paces of common shelter trench, and, say 1,200 of sections 20 or 23.

With the prospect of not more than a relief of five hours, the same sections would be used , except here and there where bits of the breastworks, 25 and 29, might be best

Thus the division might, in five hours, throw up about 1,500 paces of common trench , 1,500 of sections 20 or 23, and at the most important points 400 paces of section 29 the latter being traced to form faces and flanks

Could we calculate on two reliefs and in the ground or localities provided more cover, we might, in the first relief, use only 1,500 paces of sections 20 or 23, and with the remaining 700 sets of tools, begin 500 or 600 paces of section 32, placed in decisive situations so as to become the faces and flanks of two or three redoubts ‡ In the second relief, the 700 sets of tools might be used to complete the redoubt sections to a height of 6 ft , while, in the same relief, fresh parties would work at the gorges, and close or half close those that required it Others would make field casemates (fig. 12, pl v) in the works and help to complete the traverses, for which *tongues* would have been left.

The balance of the intrenching tools would be used in this relief to complete any cover required, in addition to that thrown up in the first relief With a third relief, 250 to 300 diggers in the redoubt ditches, would thicken the parapets to 9 or 10 feet, and others would deepen parts of the trenches and blind them with logs or rails and earth (fig. 32).

In addition, any desirable improvements in the existing shelter trenches would be carried out.

The divisional artillery would, in like manner, intrench itself according to the time available.

In the mean time, the engineers, with the infantry in support and reserve, would prepare any additional gun-pits and position gun batteries, would provide cover for the supports and reserves, and work on the communications. The

---

* It has been thought best to consider the intrenching resources of a division rather than of an army corps , for a transfer of tools from one division to another, does not seem practicable In urgent cases, however a commander might dispose of the engineers of the army corps, so as to give relief to the division or divisions on which the brunt of the work of fortifying happens to fall.

† Exclusive of the six sets to each field gun and of about 200 spades for sod cutting, which would be used with their own companies where most wanted.

‡ For this purpose the engineer tools should be used in preference , any small sets being double-manned if the soil be hard

tools available, including those of the field park, would be more numerous, in proportion to the extent of these works, than for those of the first line.

REDOUBTS, &c.

Into the details of the larger earthworks we cannot enter; but there are several questions connected with them which may be referred to. First, we see that the time and tools required, in any case limit their construction; besides which, their supposed strength draws such a fire on to them, that, unless large and well provided with splinter-proof cover, the infantry defenders may be completely silenced, or obliged to leave them, as was the case with the Duppel redoubts in 1864.

Again, as to the placing of artillery in them. In the case of isolated works, exposed on all sides, the whole of their means of defence, including guns, must be inside. When, however, it can be avoided, there are several reasons why the guns are better outside. First, the barbettes and traverses cannot be made in two or three reliefs, while the parapets can. Again, as there is not enough interior space for teams and limbers, the guns are tied to the works; while infantry can bivouac outside, and come and go quickly.

The strongest objection, however, seems to be that the attacking guns " kill two birds with one stone," for while engaged in silencing the artillery they equally disable the infantry, unless there has been time to cover the latter very effectually; while, during the close attack, the guns in redoubts are less efficient than, and are only in the way of, the infantry defenders. In fact each arm is in the wrong place during one stage of the attack.

To get over the difficulty as to* time, it has been suggested to throw up low batteries in front of the faces or flanks of redoubts, with communications through the parapets of the latter; but in the first place, the guns lose the advantage of command; while any one who has seen the glacis of a work that has been shelled, will agree that the battery would be a trap for the shells that fell short of the redoubt, while the latter, with weakened parapets, would be as much knocked about as before. The Austrian plan of having low binded pits beside the barbettes, into which the guns are run during the artillery attack, is only applicable to works thrown up at leisure; but even then, the principle of reserving the fire of the guns for the close attack is surely questionable, except in the case of works for guns only; as at this stage they will soon be silenced by the assailant's infantry, and they take up space which might be used for musketry. Under these circumstances they would, it is thought, do better service if placed some 300 or 400 yards to the rear and in flanking positions.†

It seems, therefore, that for an ordinary battle field, it will be best to intrench the guns in rear of the flanks of the redoubts, whence they may often also fire into the works if captured. Gatling guns, however, with nearly the same range as infantry, are suitable for use at the shoulders of infantry redoubts ‡

Trace.

The trace of redoubts, &c., must suit the ground and the general form of the position: when the front is most exposed it is generally shallow from front to rear. (Figs. 24 and 25, pl. VI.) Wagner points out that, if need be, the sweep of musketry from a parapet is about 30° right or left of the front. This gives some latitude in laying out the lines of a work, so as to avoid either the labour of defilading them, or the risk of their being enfiladed.

* Brielmont " Fortification Improvisée."

† Although guns were placed in most of the largest redoubts used in 1870-71 (all of which took a week to make), as a rule the artillery were in distinct positions.

‡ They only want 8 ft. length of parapet and 10 ft. to the rear.

E

Works are most secure if closed, but are more tenable if taken, and less easily retaken. Decisive works on a flank, those to be held to the last by a rear guard, and those looked into by higher positions in rear, should be closed The gorges of others, like those of advanced posts, may be secured against surprise, but not against the guns of the rear works The trace of the gorge, should provide flanking defence. Occasionally works are left quite open, so as to expose the interior spaces to musketry fire.

Size.

The size may depend on the ground or on the object of the work The garrison must be a tactical unit, numbering about one man to each pace of parapet, and, in addition, half or a third in reserve, according to the amount of secure cover for them.*

Defilade.

Works are best defiladed by their position A closed work, with faces on a crest and interior on a reverse slope, is favourably placed for defilade. High parapets only conceal , blindages alone give cover from curved fire.

Execution.

Before the working parties come up, the cutting lines of the ditches and trenches must be marked and, in place of each profile, two stout poles may be let into the ground, and cut to mark the heights of the superior and exterior crests.

The ditches are not obstacles, unless the scarps are steep† and over 7 feet high, but the defenders, if they are to succeed, will now more often repulse the attack before it nears the ditch Ditches with caponiers have been made in three short reliefs, but, unless the caponiers have space for a good number of rifles, and the bottom of the ditch can be palisaded to check the assailant, the arrangement seems hardly worth the labour. Even with **V** shaped ditches, when the usual communication has been prepared under the parapet, a Gatling pit (fig. 45, pl vii.) can be made, and the gun blinded in 3 or 4 hours after the ditch has been excavated: the fire of this gun would represent that of over 20 rifles ‡

In deep ditches, caponiers may be made somewhat like fig. 61, pl viii ; but they are much more exposed than the sunken kind.

Woods.

Woods have frequently played an important part in wars, and those of 1866 and 1870-71, furnish many examples of their influence. Woods in front, or on the flanks of a position, which give cover to the attack, are a source of great danger. On the contrary, if they are, or can be, made impassable, they diminish the area for, and the lines of, a possible advance. in woods not naturally impassable, this is best secured by felling the near border , the debouche from this, if it be 400 or 500 yards from the defenders, is generally impossible over open ground

Another important part played by woods, is to deny the use of otherwise suitable positions for the assailant's guns. Woods on the defensive zone may, if not too extensive, form advanced posts, as at Mougnot, on the Lisaine . decisive points in the shooting line, as at the bois l'Abbe by Coeuilly S E of Paris (1870-71) supporting positions, as on the road Grigny-Courcelles E of Metz (1870) , or as rear guard positions In all cases of wood defence, the great point is to hold the border and keep out the assailant. With a position including

* This agrees closely with Wagner's two men to a metre of parapet

† A scarp of 2 in 1 is impracticable, and solid earth often stands as steep as this for some time when this is not so, abatis (fig. 33, pl. vi.), is very effective.

‡ Page 23.

part of a forest on a flank, this would often lead to too great an extension, and yet the attack will try and advance through it. All that can be done, when in such a plight, is to block up, as solidly as possible, all tracks it can use, and to clear as broad a belt as possible from front to rear along the flank. This defensive border must be observed along its length, and should have a track in rear of it, along which small reserves can move, to support threatened points. This method was largely employed by the Vth German Army Corps, in the forest country S.E. of Paris (1870-71.)

In holding the borders of woods in 1870-71, the plan used, was to fell a belt along the edge (either of trees, or of their branches only if the trees were large) to bar the entrance. Obstacles were also placed some distance to the front; for those at the edge alone have this disadvantage, that if ever the assailant gets up to them, he generally does so because the defenders have fallen back, and the obstacles are therefore undefended.[*] Generally, too, shelter-trenches were used along the borders in salient positions; often half-hid among the trees so as not to draw fire. In flanking straight borders, small salient flèches outside the entanglements are so exposed to enfilade fire, that it is often best (the timber being so near) to use blinded pits (fig. 14, pl. v.) instead. These, if screened with branches, are not seen at a distance.

With large close-growing trees, the supports are safe, if so far in that they cannot see " the open" between the trunks: with small or scattered trees, cover must be made.[†] Direct and well marked tracks to the reserves were provided; these should have a bend as they approach the border, so as not to be enfiladed from the front. Guns were often brought up to the border, generally alongside a road, and were put behind pits or parapets. Blinded mitrailleur pits, screened till wanted (fig. 45, pl. vii.), are also suitable. If the border be carried, the defenders, knowing the wood, should be better able to hold together, and should use counterattacks on the flanks of the attacking parties. Gun cotton may be used to throw trees across the tracks, the defenders firing from behind abatis along the sides of them. Open spaces in the interior, and accidents of ground, such as streams, ravines, &c., may be cleared to form a retrenchment, where, behind walls or breastworks (pl. vi.), and unassailed by artillery, the defender should not fail to hold his ground.

RAILWAYS.

Apart from their strategical use as communications, and from the uses that can be made of the materials they furnish when destroyed;[‡] the features of a railway are sometimes of tactical importance. A line passing through a position from rear to front, may be an obstacle to both forces. To the front, therefore, the " over-head" bridges should be blown down, "under" bridges blocked up so as not to serve either as passages or cover; while rails should be taken up at, and obstacles placed on, the level crossings. Within the position, long cuttings may have to be bridged, and ramps made to cross embankments. In pl. i. the railway approaches the position, and then runs along the front; on this portion, the embankments would give cover to the shooting line, by notching them on the near side (fig. 10, pl. v.), when flanked by advanced villages, such as Le petit Bethoncourt, or by shelter trenches along the outer edge when unflanked.[§] In any case these embankments give cover to the supports.

* Boguslawski remarks, that the German obstacles in 1870-71 were often placed *in* and not *in front of* the defensive line.

† Young shrubs and brushwood give concealment, but do little to stop projectiles.

‡ Fig. 8, pl. v.; and figs. 49, 51, 54, and 60, pl. viii.

§ If a length of railway be unkeyed at the ends and cleared of ballast, rails and sleepers can be turned over by a row of men a pace apart (fig. 10, pl. v.)

A cutting may be used as an obstacle in front of an artillery position, or for infantry,* as in pl. II , or on sloping ground as in fig. 11, pl. V , where two tiers of fire are obtained. With the defenders on the advanced edge, the supports are covered in the cutting. To turn it, the assailant will make for the level crossings, which, however, can be well defended by reserves for the purpose near the mouths of the cuttings, and sometimes by mitrailleurs or guns concealed there   The railway in question is peculiarly favourable for the use of plated gun wagons.† These might have come into action on the curve at Héricourt   While even unblinded heavy guns on railway wagons, could have been brought up by engines or horses, and placed further south in cuttings, from the mouths or interiors of which, they could have fired (under cover) along the Lisaine, and have enfiladed the ground in front of the position   The curves, too, in a line, can often be turned to account to increase the sweep of the guns, which should have besides, a traversing arrangement of their own on the wagons ‡

RIVERS.

The use of rivers, as obstacles, has already been referred to.   In the late American and French wars, large rivers like the Seine and Loire, and some of those in America, were used for gun boats to take part in the operations.

Ready-made casemates for these are often furnished by the bridges, and even if exposed, 2-inch plating renders them safe against field shells   If the assailant have any gunboats, the defender lays down torpedoes, and sinks vessels across the channel, flanking the obstacles with works on the bank.§

COVER FOR GUNS.

The general artillery positions having been chosen, it remains to improve or make cover for the guns‖   The sites for the pits or batteries are safer, if they have steep pitches just in front, which catch projectiles, (fig. 30, pl. VI): the guns, too, then stand higher than the shooting line, and fire over it.   The benefit is greatest, when the shell fire directed on the shooting line, is at short ranges ; for then its effects may extend 500 or 600 paces to the rear of that line   Guns on the level of the shooting line, are more exposed to these effects; and besides, require gaps, to fire through, in the parts which are in front of them.

The *division* of 10 men with each field gun has 6 picks and 6 shovels, and can often intrench its own gun , but it is desirable also to have additional epaulments ready to meet the contingencies of the fight¶   Accidents of ground will sometimes give cover in either of the ways shewn (fig. 47, pl. VII), or a crest may be notched (fig 35) so as just to fire over it.

Cover can always be obtained by sinking the guns, or putting them behind breastworks.   The first method is the quicker and less laborious , but the terre-

---

* At the battle of Nuits (1870-71) the Germans suffered severely in attacking a cutting held by the French —' Le Général Crémer "   See also pl III

† Railway wagons were used in four of the sorties before Paris in 1870-71. None were disabled, though their 2 in plating was often struck   Breech-loaders are required for railway wagons.

‡ In deliberate preparations, the service traction engines would be available to haul on roads or railroads, as well as for sawing, &c

§ The Seine was thus barricaded below Rouen (1870-71.)—GŒTZE   " Thätigkeit der deutschen ingenieui."

‖ Of the 102 guns in first line on the Lisaine, all but three or four batteries were intrenched   As to protection, the guns so covered lost in the three days fighting, on an average, less than four men in each field battery —WENGEN

¶ Thus on la Grange Dame, reserve gun-pits were made for the two field batteries, which at first stood at the old citadel and by Montbéliard —LOHLEIN.

plein may be wet and is generally softer than the natural crust ; nor will the guns always have the necessary command.*

Our present pattern of pit does well for B L. guns or mitrailleurs ; but it is too short for 16-pr. M.L. guns, the recoil of which is 16 or 17 feet on the level. As to the relative merits of breech and muzzle-loaders, artillerymen are the proper judges : those on the continent fancy that a breech-loader with a chamber which burns a charge of mild powder, does the same work with less recoil, and so may be fought on a lighter carriage, and can be intrenched and worked in a less space.†

Construction.

To be quickly used, gun-pits must be simple in trace and make. A number of ways of covering field guns and guns of position are shown in pl. VII. For guns opposed only to field artillery, it does not seem necessary to have parapets thicker than 9 to 12 feet, as most of the damage to them is done by shells pitching within 3 or 4 feet of the superior crest, and against this, additional thickness is of little use. Indeed the enormous effect of shrapnel with time fuzes, makes height to cover the detachments the more important point. Unfortunately, with our carriages for position-guns, we must either fire through embrasures or over low parapets, as with field guns, and when much sweep is required, the latter seem best ; but, by way of protection, some of the available sand bags should be placed as moveable bonnettes on the fronts of the gun batteries, thick turfs, fascines, &c., being used for the field guns.

Protection and Concealment of Guns.

When space permits, gun-pits may be placed 25 to 30 paces apart or more. Important groups, or those much exposed, should be secured from a sudden rush, by obstacles or other slight defences. Occasionally in exposed artillery positions, storm-proof redoubts, for guns alone, may be required. The supporting infantry will generally be in shelter-trenches cn the flanks. Flanking guns, exposed on one side only, may be placed alongside a parapet, like that in fig 36 (only higher and longer), and in the trench, which should be at least 6 feet wide. It is often important to hide the guns till they open fire. Trees partly cut through or prepared with gun-cotton may be thrown down when required. Hedges cut down in clearing the front may be replanted, and even snow parapets used for the purpose. Again, epaulments may be both supported and concealed by hedges (fig. 47, pl. VII); portions of tall hedges may be cut through, and pulled out when going to fire. If no other screen can be got, the principle of the earth screen, so happily introduced for siege batteries, may be used with or without gun-pits.

Platforms.

For guns of position, platforms must be improvised. Heavy logs laid horizontally, act as sleepers, roof and floor joists being fixed to them with spikes or trenails, or a plank and two wedges (fig. 39) will answer the purpose.‡

Limber Pits.

Limber pits should not be placed directly in rear of the guns, as was sometimes done in 1870-71. Our pattern of pit, across the range, seems as good as any, but limber-pits are seldom wanted ; as small magazines, by the gun-pits (pl. VII.), where ammunition can be stored in boxes, barrels, &c., are often more convenient in exposed places.

* Some of the emplacements used in 1870-71, were simply walls of turf 3 ft high and thick.

† The German field gun-pit for B.L. is only 13 ft. long in the terreplein. — WAGNER.

‡ Even a couple of railway sleepers, bedded under the wheels, are useful.

Gatling Gun Pits.

As Gatling guns have no recoil, the wheels and trail may be sunk ; or pits, traced as in fig 45, and 2 feet deep, may be made, each by 5 men, in an hour When timber can be got, these may be deepened and blinded Rails are even better than timber for roofing purposes (fig 49, pl VIII)*

COVER FOR SUPPORTS AND RESERVES

The cover for the supports, and sometimes for the reserves, differs in this respect from other cover,† namely, that the troops may not require to shoot from it. The thin shooting line, though much exposed, offers but a small target, while bodies in support, in the open, would suffer much more Formerly, in the Peninsula for example, a shallow trench and parapet gave enough cover to troops behind it , but now, on account of the increased drop of the long ranging projectiles in use, and the severity of the opening fire, such cover is hardly sufficient One of the chief lessons of the war of 1870 71, is the use that was made of blindages, or *field casemates*, for the supports, when exposed to heavy fire, and when timber or rails were procurable. When sub-soil water is not met with, these are best made *sunken*, as the low roofs are more easily concealed and offer less of a mark. The methods that seem to have answered best are indicated in figs 3, 4, 7, 12, and 13, pl v , and fig. 43, pl VIII ‡

The posts for the reserves should, if possible, be unseen from the front, so as not to be exposed to the assailant's distant fire. When so exposed, earthworks are often best.

SECOND AND THIRD LINES.

Except when there is much time for preparation, as was the case before Metz in 1870, and Paris in 1870-71, second and third lines, it is thought, will now be less used , the holding of the first or shooting line being all-important. Portions of such lines, consisting of localities or earthworks § may be used in *support* of the first line, when situated facing the spaces between the decisive points in that line, and 800 to 1,000 paces to the rear of them , or they may be placed directly in rear of these points, and at about half the above distances, so as to *command* them.

OBSTACLES.

Obstacles are most valuable in a close country, and where the field for fire is small. The formations for attack are now less impeded by obstacles , but with the necessity for increased extension, their value has increased, as a means of neutralising certain areas over which the assailant might advance, and of defining the lines of advance For this purpose they are used any distance to the front, within the limits of the defender's fire.

Along the offensive zone, if placed rather further forward than the position the assailant strives to reach for the fire contest with the defender's infantry,|| the latter, with rather a greater effective range, can still command them,¶ and

---

* Mitrailleurs do not injure their own embrasures as guns do.

† It is perhaps to be regretted that we have not given the names "shelter-trenches" to those for cover only, and " shooting-trenches" to those from which men fire

‡ In all timber work of this kind wooden trenails act as tenons, and supply the place of spikes the 2 in pocket augurs are invaluable for this work. When the earth is not solid board or hurdle revetments keep it up, and increase the cover given by the parapet

§ Such were the Paulus and Semacourt redoubts before Metz . the latter with good casemates

|| Distant, as we have already seen, about 200 to 400 paces from the defenders , hence these obstacles might be a little over 300 yards forward

¶ In firing standing at 300 yards, the M H. bullet, aimed at a man's middle, only rises to 6 ft. 9 in. and grazes at 360 yards.

obstacles so placed, leave a clear field for counter-attack in front of the shooting-line.

Along the defensive zone, the obstacles before decisive points are perfectly commanded, if between 50 and 200 paces forward. Those closing the intervals may be either retired like a curtain, with 50 yard gaps close to the decisive points, through which the reserves debouch; or they may be so far to the front, as to give the latter room to strike the assailants as they close.

The text books deal with the nature and details of obstacles and the conditions they have to fulfil. We may remark, however, in the first place, that obstacles, which with little labour cover a large area, are now most valuable. They should also be capable of resisting the powerful rush of men.

Timber makes the best obstacle, whether as abatis or entanglements, and when it is plentiful and on the spot, quantity is more important than quality. No amount of artillery fire will destroy a broad belt of abatis,* nor does it burn when green.

Next to abatis, wire entanglements are most generally useful, but wire cannot often be found; nor, unfortunately, do we carry it in the field.† It is fastened "knee high" above ground to several rows of stout, strongly driven stakes, placed chequerwise, and 7 to 10 feet apart, or to stumps of trees.

Pointed stakes, if strong, answer all the purposes of shallow pits, and are very quickly driven and then sharpened.‡ Our Chinese experience showed the value of these.

Barricades, when unavoidably exposed to artillery, should be very solid, and of earth, paving stones, or timber. They should (figs. 26 and 27, pl. vi.) have gaps both for sorties and retreat. When a road is barricaded in front of a position, abatis is best, as a parapet gives cover to the assailant.

Fougasses or mines may be fired either mechanically or chemically, when trodden on; and occasionally by§ electricity (by observation or contact). They are chiefly valuable in defending mountain passes, where small charges may be used to start avalanches of stones, which, once in motion, keep going of themselves. Against night attacks, too, certain kinds are useful.

By means of dams, a stream may be made impassable, or a hollow flooded. Thus, in 1871, the bed of the Lisaine was deepened,‖ and two dams, to raise the water level, were made, one above Montbéliard, and the other against the broken bridge of Bethoncourt. The latter was of dung, and formed a foot bridge to little Bethoncourt. The left front of Stains (pl. ii.) was also inundated.

Stockades are often useful as barriers or screens¶, when earth could not be raised so high (fig. 51, pl. viii.), sometimes also as a parapet. Guns cannot breach them easily; thus, in New Zealand, an 8 in. gun, two 24-pr. howitzers, and a 9-pr., were fired for two hours, at a native stockade (fig. 31, pl. vi.), and failed to breach it at 200 yards' range, because the shells passed through before bursting; and it took over an hour to do so at 900 yards' range, with six 12-pr. B.L.R. guns. Rockets, with gun-cotton bursters, seem likely to be effective in such cases.

* Belts of abatis 150 paces wide, were used in 1870-71, before Metz and Paris.

† A mile of 14 B.W.G. wire, which answers for this and for siege purposes, weighs only 90 lbs.: weight for weight, perhaps the most useful material we could carry. Telegraph wire (No. 8) is better, but is five times as heavy and very stiff.

‡ Each R.E. Company has 13 draw-knives for the purpose: sharpened sword-bayonets may be used.

§ For the first, the small-arm gun-lock, and the artillery friction tube are the means most often available: for the last, there is a dynamo-electric machine with each R.E. Company.

‖ This can only be done in water less than knee-deep.—WAGNER.

¶ Stockades of vertical fascines make very tall screens with little trouble, and if well connected, resist explosives extremely well.

NIGHT ATTACKS.

It may not be out of place to refer here, to the growing importance of *night attacks.* The subject is now receiving much attention on the continent, and in the war of 1870-71, the Germans, thanks to their own high discipline, and to the bad patrolling of the French, were in these operations constantly successful * The method used, was to combine a front attack, with another taking the front in reverse, and as the defender, at night, loses much of his superiority of fire, such attacks are very serious. To guard against surprise, when in the presence of the enemy, troops must be bivouaced near the defences they are to hold, so as to assemble, on the first warning, at their proper *alarm posts*, and man the works previously occupied by sentries. The outposts should be numerous, and the ground should be carefully patrolled well to the front, particularly before dawn, signalling parties, with lamps, may advance in rear of the patrols, and report hostile movements. Wire entanglements, with bells, were used by the Germans in 1870-71, to prevent an enemy from approaching unheard. The possible lines of advance, should be limited by obstacles and closed by wire, which may be used to fire fougasses, some of which, may also be arranged to explode when trodden on These, however small,† would produce much moral and some material effect, as the assailant must move in close order , for which reason, also, guns (to fire case) and mitrailleurs should be laid to sweep particular lines of advance. To judge when to shoot, and to let the infantry see the ground, the outposts, in retiring, light fires, with screens towards the defenders ,‡ and lime-lights may occasionally be posted in salient positions, so as, at critical moments, to light up the fore-ground for several hundred yards, while the defenders are in darkness §

COMMUNICATIONS IN REAR

The work of *" clearing for action "* for defence divides itself into—

(1.) The widening and improving of existing roads||, and the making of new roads, and occasionally of bits of railroads,¶ and of platforms for unloading.

(2.) The making of bridges and ramps, or the making out of fords at all breaks in the communications**.

(3) The mining of bridges, which may have to be blown up along the lines of retreat

For the first, all impediments, such as fences or walls, are cut or knocked down. In woods, the underwood is cleared away for infantry, and trees cut down and roots grubbed up for gun tracks. Swamps are *corduroyed* or made good with fascines ††

* Thus before Belfort, in 1870 71 Danjoutin and Perouse were taken with small loss though Vinoy mentions that the Germans failed to retake Ville-Evrart by a night attack. because the supports fired into the advance. The French failed in two night attacks on the Lisaine. They succeeded at Noisseville and Flanville (Metz, 1870)

† Fougasses of light balls or carcasses would light up the ground just when wanted.

‡ Petroleum on hay or straw burns brightly, and would last long enough to show a column at hand

§ Our telegraph troop can send out at least four parties with lanterns, and has eight lime-lights only half a troop, however, accompanies each army corps

|| Werder s troops had to lay sand and dung on the ice-covered roads, up which they took their guns on the 14th of January, 1871.

¶ Before Metz, for example, in 1870.

** In this, the pontoon troop, with each army corps, would generally assist.

†† Lieut Col Home mentions, that 200 men to a mile was found the best strength for road-making parties in Ashantee, in 1874.

In making communications, it should be remembered that, for rapid movements, troops should move with as large a front as possible; hence the communications should be wide, but as the width of the narrowest bridge or defile may limit the front all through, it will often be useless to make some parts wider than others, except where sidings are wanted to allow traffic to pass both ways.

Tracks may be marked out by *blazed* trees, and directions should be chalked up on walls or boards, to point out the way at all junctions.

FIELD TELEGRAPHS.

The tactical use of the field telegraph, as applied to a position, is to keep the commander acquainted with the state of things all along the line," and to enable him to direct his reserves, and judge the moment for counter-attacks. The system used in 1870-71 before Paris and Metz, was to run the main wires from head-quarters along the line of the reserves, with branches to important forward stations.

Thus, with the resources of two English telegraph half troops,† a commander, at Brevilliers, might (pl. 1.) be in telegraphic communication with both flanks of the Lisaine position, with Delle and Beaucourt, and with the besieger's head-quarters at Bourogne; whence, by a semi-permanent line to Mühlhausen, he would be connected with the head-quarters before Paris. The branch line to Bavillard, enables him to call on the siege troops to support his right flank; while the stations on Mont Vaudois and l'Ordon Brisée, with the signallers where shown,‡ would inform him of the progress of the fight along the front.§ The station on the Ronchamps road and that facing Mandeure, are meant for lime-lights, and should be withdrawn to *pre-arranged* points before the outposts are driven in.

FIELD OBSERVATORIES.

Observatories may be made, when steeples, heights, &c., do not give a good view of the front. They are mostly used with telegraph or signalling stations, and have signalling telescopes. Platforms in tree-tops, or on scaffolding, or single derricks can be used; these may be hid behind woods, over the tops of which the observer can look.||

MEASUREMENT OF RANGES.

Every one agrees that the distances to important points should be measured. Without a few hours of daylight little can be done in this way. The field batteries have now the means of finding their own ranges;¶ but the ranges from position batteries and from cover prepared beforehand, should be measured beforehand too. Each R.E. company has a theodolite and chain, and, in day-

---

* The lines of Torres Vedras were furnished with a system of semaphore stations.

† Each half troop carries 18 miles of wire, and provides 6 telegraph stations, 2 to 3 double parties of signallers, and 4 lime-lights.

‡ For distances under two miles, it is safest to use relays of orderlies, as was actually done in this case. The flags work up to three or four miles, and may, in such cases, save time.

§ Since this essay was written, it has been ascertained that a field telegraph was used, on the occasion of the fight, from Frahir through Brévilliers to Bourogne and Delle. The French struck it at Frahir.—WENGEN.

|| For heights not over 50 ft. they can be raised in a night. They have been made as high as 160 feet.

¶ Nolan's range-finder, approved for our field artillery, can now be used both with and away from the guns.

light, officers who are constructing batteries, should take the most important measurements In the same way the engineer officer with each section of the infantry defences, can use a pocket sextant, to measure such ranges as may be required * In both cases, the ranges should be written up, and the points shown to the officers concerned.

REARGUARD POSITIONS.

In order to provide against every contingency, the positions to be held by the rearguards, in case of retreat, should be fixed upon   These will command the lines of retreat, and should, in any case, be at least so far behind the shooting line, as not to be silenced by musketry fire from that line if taken , their situation should be such as will best prevent the assailant from commanding the retreat with his guns.   Fortified localities answer well , in default of them, *closed* earthworks may be used

CONCLUSIONS.

We see, therefore, that when but one or two hours are available, trenches can be dug, localities can be hastily barricaded, their immediate fronts cleared a little, walls notched, banquettes formed, windows built up, and communications made, where most wanted   With woods, the salient parts of the borders can be felled for entanglements, and bits of shelter trenches thrown up , while pits and epaulments can be made for some of the guns and mitrailleurs. With a night available for work, it is all important that the directing officer should decide, *before dark*, on what is to be done   After this, the parties are hastily organized and all the available lanterns† are distributed , the clearing of the front is persevered in , strong barricades are made in the villages , the outer shooting lines are strengthened, and gaps in them closed by breastworks, stockades, and hurdle walls.   The angles of walls and flanking portions are loopholed , houses are prepared for defence, and epaulments for infantry thrown up on the flanks , while in exposed places, shelter-trenches are made for the shooting line, and a few blindages are provided for the supports, and preparations made for the reserves , the communications along the rear are improved, and those in front impeded   Additional cover is provided for the guns, and working parties are employed for a relief, in intrenching any guns of position.   The field telegraph is also laid‡ and organized

If two reliefs be available in the night, a few large infantry redoubts may be thrown up , obstacles may be placed along the front with some care , and the positions for the reserves put into a state of preparation. In this way a good deal can be done, but in the dark it will be done imperfectly

When one or even many days are available, the works indicated above are continually improved upon. A more extended use is made of obstacles ; the front is carefully cleared, and the communications along the rear further opened out The villages and localities are divided into defensive sections, exposed positions defiladed by traverses, and long walls flanked by tambours.   Field casemates are made for the supports, and the reserves are further intrenched, if need be, in infantry re-

* The method of tangents is the simplest in the field   With the theodolite, the difference of level can be taken at the same time as the range   the sextant gives good results up to 1000 yards.

† Each R E. company has only four lanterns , a few can be got from other services.

‡ The rate of reeling out being from two to three miles an hour for each wagon.

doubts.   Second lines of defence may be begun and prepared as time permits. *

It is true that the defender may sometimes calculate on having many days or weeks for work, and in such cases, in open country particularly, he might occupy the ground systematically with powerful casemated works, similar to those thrown up for the defence of Washington, in 1861-2 ; and round Dresden and Vienna in 1866, where rails were largely used in making bomb-proof cover (fig. 54, pl. VIII.)

Such works, with palisades and caponiers in the ditches, and with temporary haxo-casemates (figs. 59 and 60) for the guns, and hollow traverses for the defenders (figs. 56 and 62) could offer so great a resistance, that an assailant might have to become a besieger.

A battle field is more often prepared (to use a homely phrase) " from hand to mouth" : the defender not knowing what the next day may have in store.   In such cases we must do the best we can, in the time we are sure of, remembering that at every stage, the work must be ready for the fight.

And now a word about the troops, compared with whom, these works are but the husk of the defence.

Since the days of Thermopylae the defence, though the less brilliant part, has always called for the highest virtues of the soldier ; and yet the popular notion is, that for such a purpose any troops are good enough.   This idea, always false, is now more so than ever.   Over and over again in 1871, we saw the French, individually brave and apt at using cover, unable, for lack of discipline, to hold their positions against inferior numbers of the invader ; while the superiority of the latter on the defensive was equally marked.   To discipline alone, is due the faith in self and in each other, which gives coolness in action, and with it the power of straight shooting and of orderly movement ; the willingness to bear hardship with patience, and do irksome work when called upon, and above all the determination to *stay,* which no hammering can overcome, and for which our people have been always famous.

To discipline must be added, *readiness* both for war and in war.   In former days, when war was the business of life, success depended on being " ever ready " to follow up words by deeds.   In these days of " deeds without words " the inventions of science, in the hands of armed nations, may crowd the incidents of a war into the space of a few weeks, and readiness that comes of forethought, is the only safeguard.

"Nullum numen habes, si sit prudentia : nos te,"

" Nos facimus, Fortuna, deam, cœloque locamus"

is more true now, than when it was the watchword of the great nation, which, longer than all others, held the mastery in war ; and which, with a temple to Fortune, left nothing to chance.

* As a practical comment on hasty preparation, the defences at Héricourt may be referred to.   It will be seen that, before the town, the wood du Chanois stretched across the hill of Mougnot, a sort of pleasure ground covered with large trees.   These would have concealed an advance from Tavey, which thus could have taken the hill and used it against the town.   The Germans therefore worked night and day to clear away the wood.   This they finished, except in the northern part.   The foot of the hill was protected by abatis ; the old hollow road barricaded, and shelter-trenches and gun-pits for a battery thrown up on the high ground.   To the north, the chapel of St. Valbert and the stone walls of the churchyard were occupied, and flanked the front of Mougnot ; and the farm of Marion, surrounded by abatis, formed a keep to it.   To the south, shelter-trenches were thrown up along the great road to Bussurel, and supported by a defended factory on the left bank.   The western enclosure walls of Héricourt were provided with banquettes, and the windows of the houses looking west were blocked up and loopholed.

A. W. AND J. P. JACKSON, PRINTERS, THOMAS STREET, WOOLWICH.

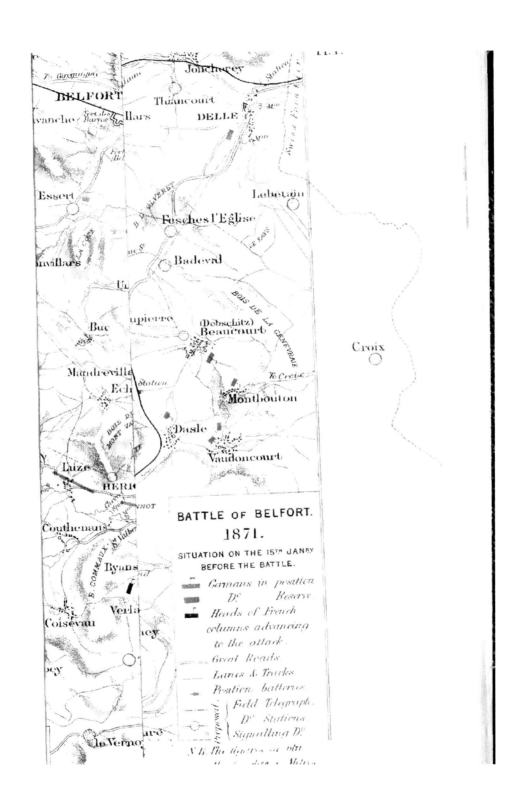

BATTLE OF BELFORT.
1871.

SITUATION ON THE 15TH JAN.RY
BEFORE THE BATTLE.

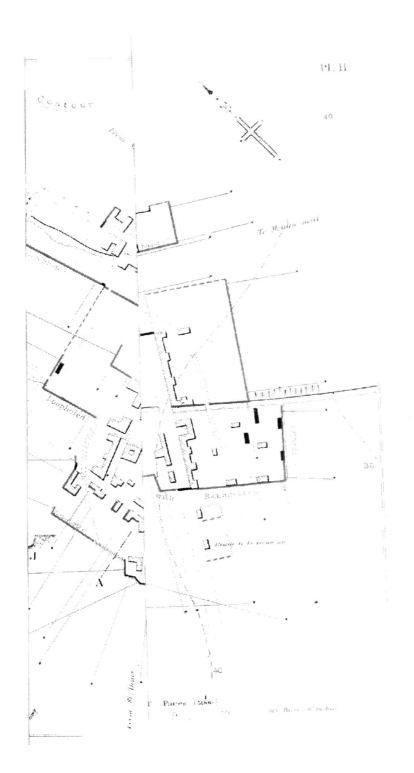

Pl. II

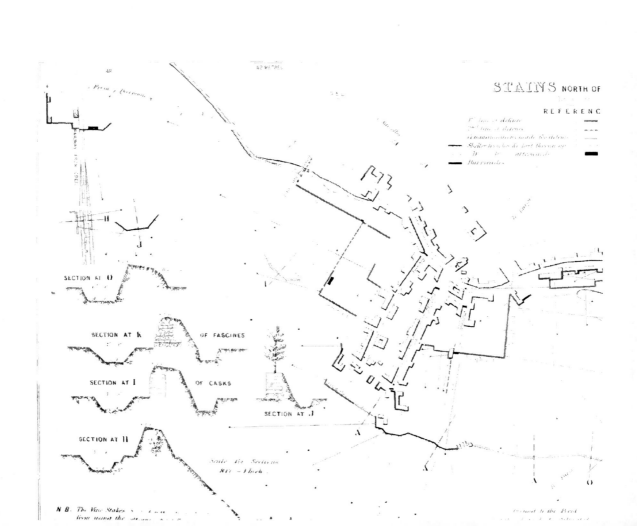

STAINS NORTH OF

REFERENC

SECTION AT O

SECTION AT K   OF FASCINES

SECTION AT I   OF CASKS

SECTION AT J

SECTION AT II

-

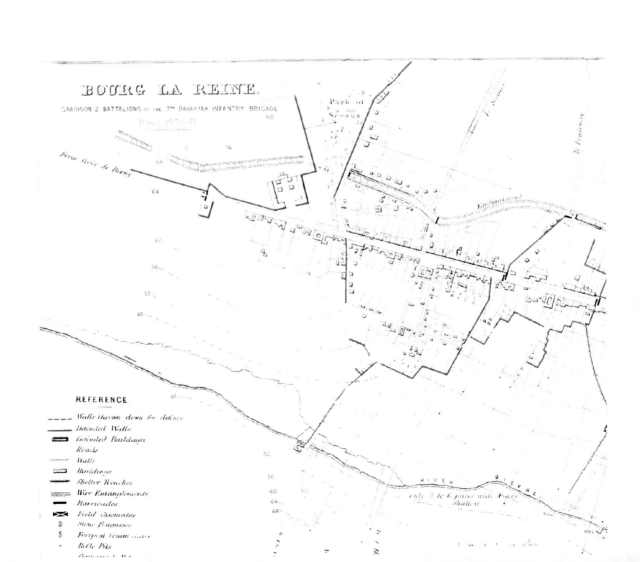

BOURG LA REINE.

GARRISON 2 BATTALIONS OF THE 7TH BAVARIAN INFANTRY BRIGADE

Plan 1870-71

Park of
Sceaux

From Croix de Berny

Embankment

RIVER   BIEVRE

only 3 to 6 paces wide but very
shallow

REFERENCE

----	Walls thrown down for defence
———	Defended Walls
▬▬	Defended Buildings
	Roads
·······	Walls
⬭	Buildings
∿∿∿	Shelter Trenches
▦▦▦	Wire Entanglements
▬	Barricades
⧓	Field Casemates
▣	Stone Enclosures
8	Forepost Commander
·	Rifle Pits

Pl. IV.

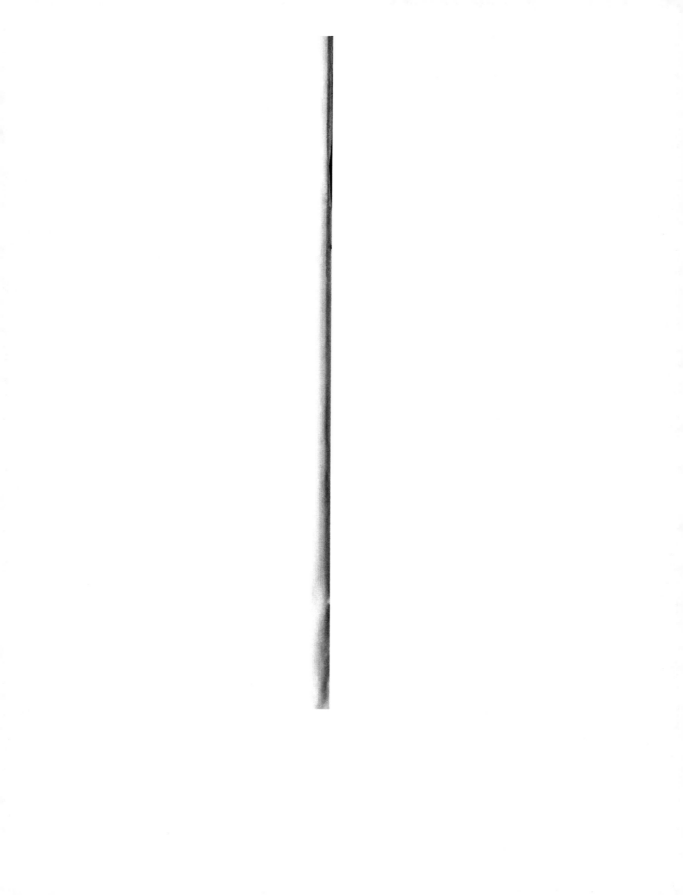

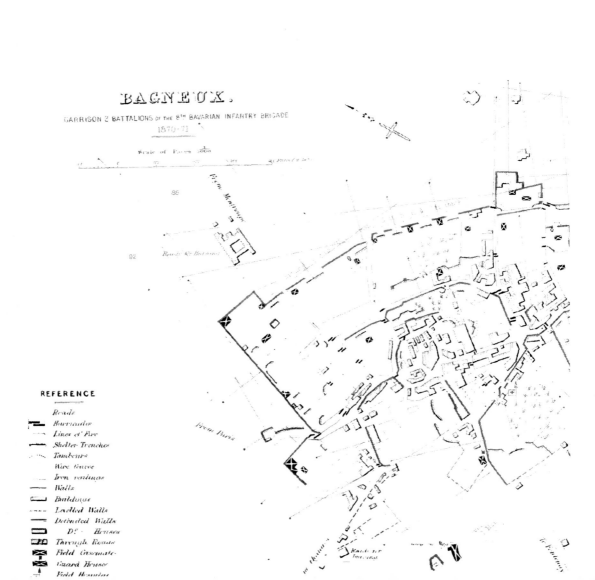

BAGNEUX.

GARRISON 2 BATTALIONS OF THE 8TH BAVARIAN INFANTRY BRIGADE

1870-71

Scale of Paces 2500

REFERENCE

Roads
Barricades
Lines of Fire
Shelter Trenches
Tambours
Wire Fence
Iron verlings
Walls
Buildings
Loopholed Walls
Defended Walls
D.º Houses
Through Roads
Field Casemate
Guard House
Field Hospital

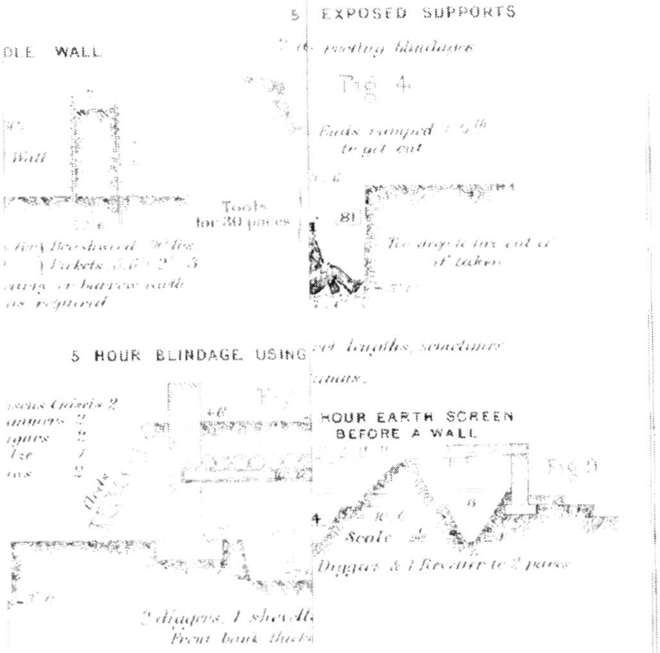

5 EXPOSED SUPPORTS

...resting blindage

Fig 4

...WALL

Wall

Ends ramped ... ...th
to get out

Tools
for 30 paces

...ho drop to turn out of
... ...at taken

... ...shaped ... ...
... Pickets ...
... ...barrow earth
as required

5 HOUR BLINDAGE USING ... lengths, sometimes

...anas.

HOUR EARTH SCREEN
BEFORE A WALL

Fig ...

...Cutters 2
...augers 2
...gers 2
...ze ...
...ns ...

Scale ...

Diggers & 1 Recorder to 2 paces

2 diggers 1 shovell...
Front bank thick...

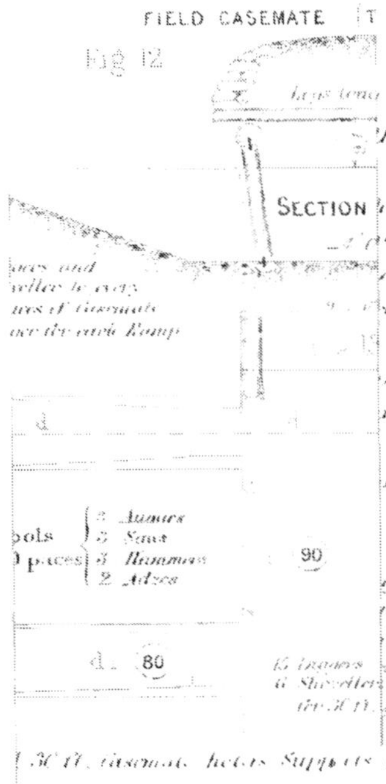

FIELD CASEMATE ...

Fig 12

READ.

the diggers for this and the
...lowing plates are supposed to
...at 2 paces interval unless
...erwise stated The arrows
...ow the direction of thro...
...figures enclosed thus ____
... ...re the number of Square feet
... a Section

SECTION

...se enclosed thus ◯ are the
...number of Cube feet in a task

...de for all the figures,
Except N° 11, 56

...pers and
...uller to carry
...ues of Casemate
...are for each Ramp

...gs 3 & 7. every second upright has a pair
...uts Iron dogs would be used with the
...k when procurable The number of
...diggers ... would be decided on, on the spot
...to Shovellers
...ts shown Plates V to VIII ... are only an ...
...the available material would, in each

ols ⎰ 2 Augers
⎱ 3 Saws
paces ⎰ 5 Rammers
⎱ 2 Adzes

90

d. 80

...1 30 ft. casemate, hetcs Supports used

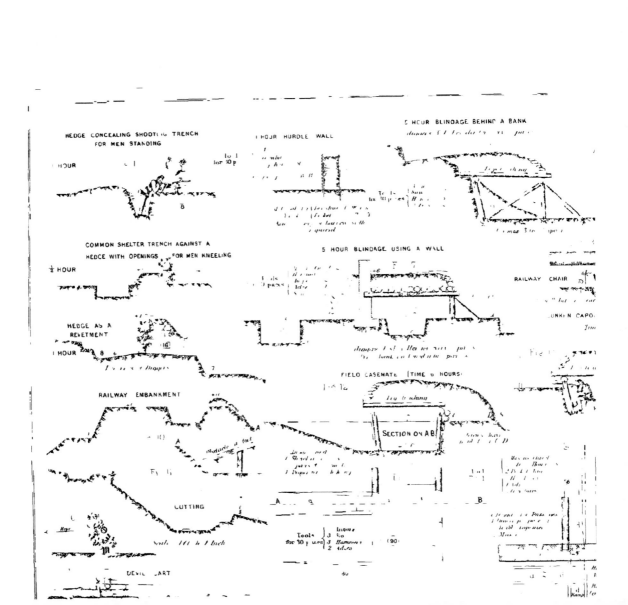

HEDGE CONCEALING SHOOTING TRENCH
FOR MEN STANDING

I HOUR

I HOUR HURDLE WALL

5 HOUR BLINDAGE BEHIND A BANK

COMMON SHELTER TRENCH AGAINST A
HEDGE WITH OPENINGS   FOR MEN KNEELING

½ HOUR

5 HOUR BLINDAGE USING A WALL

RAILWAY CHAIR

HEDGE AS A
REVETMENT

I HOUR

FIELD CASEMATE (TIME 6 HOURS)

SECTION ON AB

RAILWAY EMBANKMENT

CUTTING

Tools
for 30 p ure

DEVIL CART

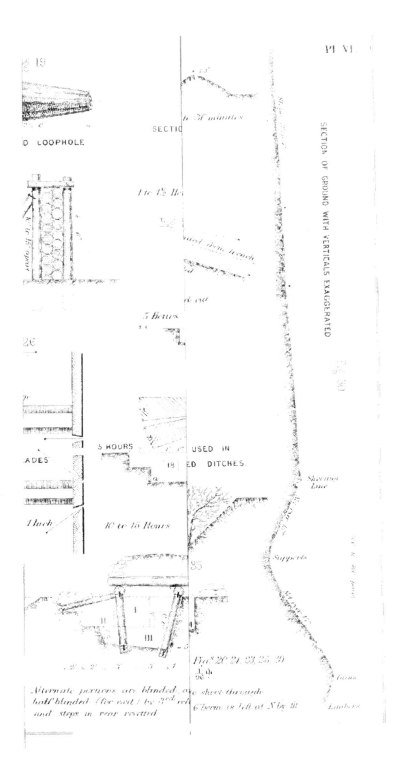

PL VI

SECTION OF GROUND WITH VERTICALS EXAGGERATED

D LOOPHOLE

SECTIO

to 30 minutes

1 to 1½ Ho

5 Hours

5 HOURS   USED IN
IB ED DITCHES.

ADES

1 Inch

10 to 15 Hours

Shooting
line

Supports

Carres

Limbers

Fig.ⁿ 20 21 23 25 29

Alternate portions are blinded, one sheet through
half blinded (for exit) by 3ʳᵈ ect   6 berm is left at 8 by 9
and steps in rear revetted

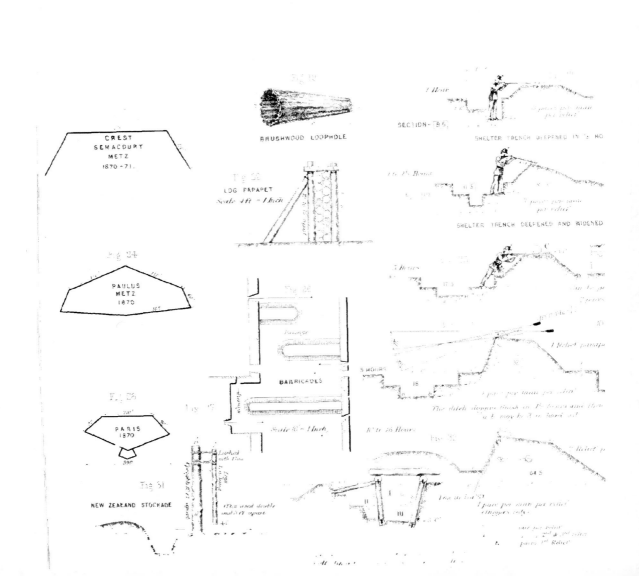

CREST
SEMACOURT
METZ
1870-71.

BRUSHWOOD LOOPHOLE

Fig. ??
LOG PARAPET
Scale 4ft = 1 Inch

SECTION - ??
SHELTER TRENCH DEEPENED IN ½ HO...

SHELTER TRENCH DEEPENED AND WIDENED

PAULUS
METZ
1870

PARIS
1870

BARRICADES

Scale 16 = 1 Inch.

NEW ZEALAND STOCKADE

7. 6'

A. + 4.
MAGAZINE

B

reef with 6 ft. leas
& widen it to 6 ft.,
pits & ramp their ends
ake the Shelter pits

½ HOUR PIT FOR HE

A

56

9 Diggers
5 Revetters
3 Shovellers

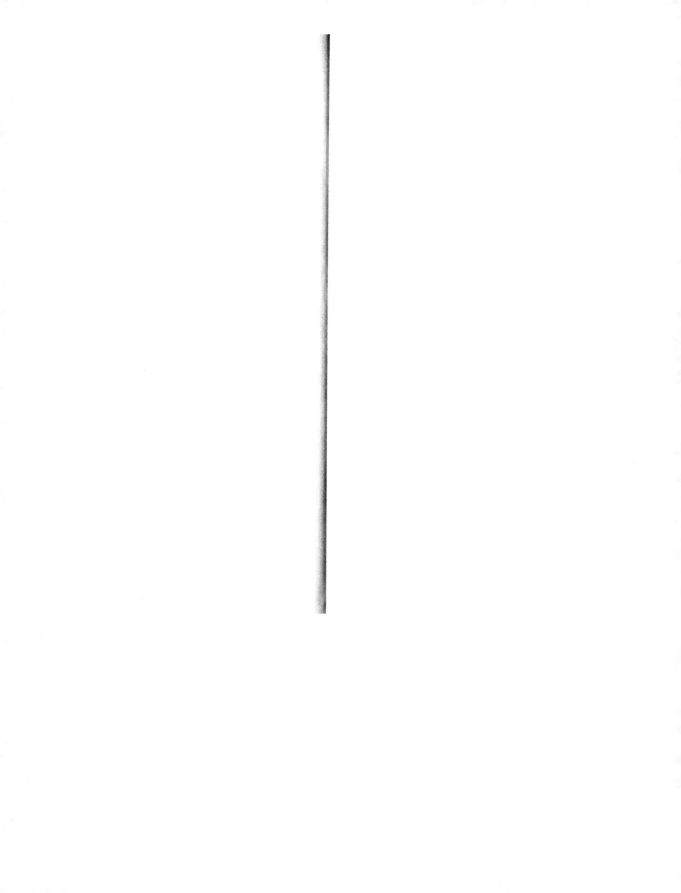

ONE HOUR ... LAN ...

ONE HOUR EPAULMENT OR EXPOSED LARKS

ONE HOUR EPAULMENT

SECTION ON ...

S H LR SUR ACE BA.TERY
FOR GUNS OF POSITION

WORKING PARTIES ... 41	WORKIN PARTIES ... 42

3 HOURS SUNKEN BATTERY
F R GUNS O POSITION

SECTION ... LINE OF FIRE

SECTION ON A.B.

Fig. 54.

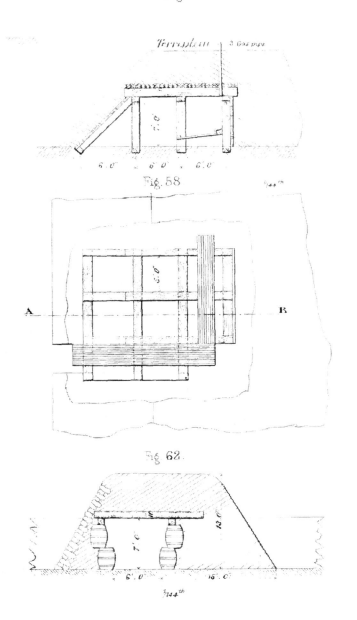

Fig. 58.

A   B

Fig. 62.

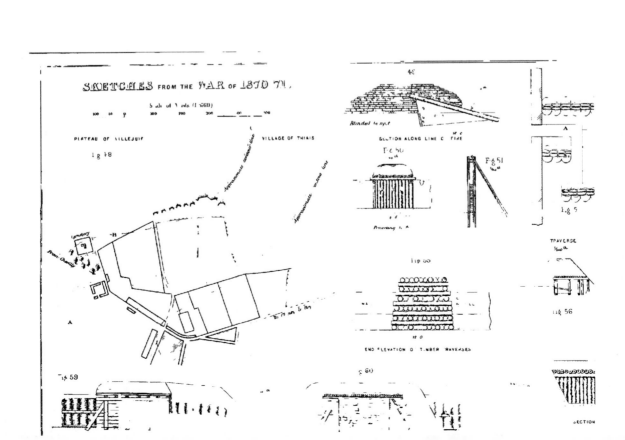

SKETCHES from the WAR of 1870 71.

Scale of Yards (1:500)

PLATEAU OF VILLEJUIF

Fig 48

VILLAGE OF THIAIS

48

Blinded loophole

SECTION ALONG LINE C FIRE

Fig 50

Fig 51

A

Fig 5

TRAVERSE

Fig 55

Fig 56

Fig 59

Fig 60

END ELEVATION OF TIMBER TRAVERSES

SECTION

）

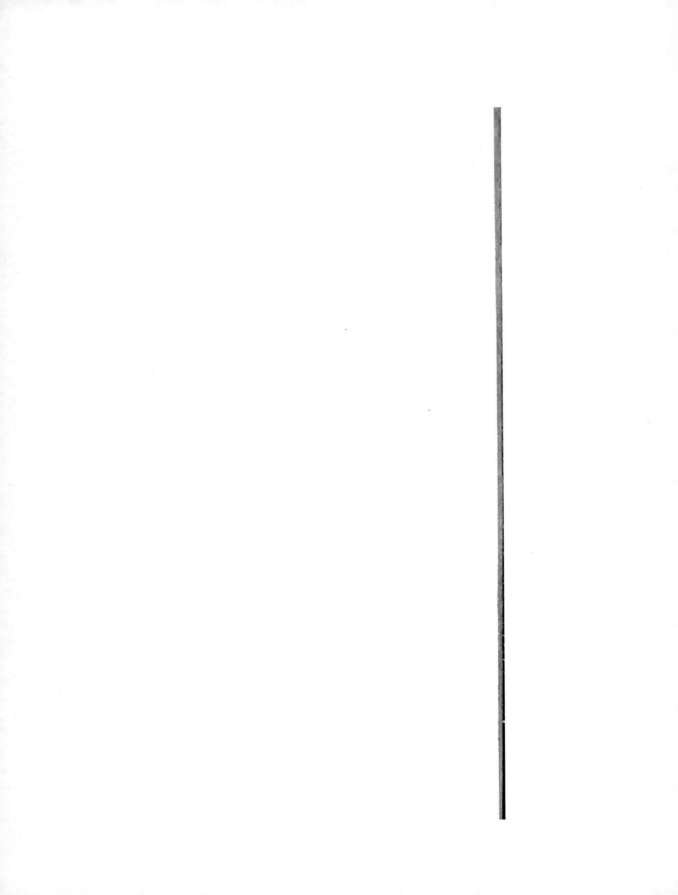

CPSIA information can be obtained at www.ICGtesting.com
Printed in the USA
BVOW02s1150190315

392427BV00013BA/146/P